P9-DNG-202

COLLEGEVILLE BIBLE COMMENTARY

THE GOSPEL

ACCORDING TO

MARK

Philip Van Linden, C.M.

THE LITURGICAL PRESS

Collegeville, Minnesota

ABBREVIATIONS

Gen—Genesis
Exod—Exodus
Lev—Leviticus
Num—Numbers
Deut—Deuteronomy
Josh—Joshua
Judg—Judges
Ruth—Ruth
1 Sam—1 Samuel
2 Sam—2 Samuel
1 Kgs—1 Kings
2 Kgs—2 Kings
1 Chr—1 Chronicles
2 Chr—2 Chronicles
Ezra—Ezra
Neh—Nehemiah
Tob—Tobit
Jdt—Judith
Esth—Esther
1 Macc—1 Maccabees
2 Macc—2 Maccabees
Job—Job
Ps(s)—Psalms(s)
Prov—Proverbs

Eccl—Ecclesiastes
Song—Song of Songs
Wis—Wisdom
Sir—Sirach
Isa—Isaiah
Jer—Jeremiah
Lam—Lamentations
Bar—Baruch
Ezek—Ezekiel
Dan—Daniel
Hos—Hosea
Joel—Joel
Amos—Amos
Obad—Obadiah
Jonah—Jonah
Mic—Micah
Nah—Nahum
Hab—Habakkuk
Zeph—Zephaniah
Hag—Haggai
Zech—Zechariah
Mal—Malachi
Matt—Matthew
Mark—Mark
Luke—Luke

John—John
Acts—Acts
Rom—Romans
1 Cor—1 Corinthians
2 Cor—2 Corinthians
Gal—Galatians
Eph—Ephesians
Phil—Philippians
Col—Colossians
1 Thess—1 Thessalonians
2 Thess—2 Thessalonians
1 Tim—1 Timothy
2 Tim—2 Timothy
Titus—Titus
Phlm—Philemon
Heb—Hebrews
Jas—James
1 Pet—1 Peter
2 Pet—2 Peter
1 John—1 John
2 John—2 John
3 John—3 John
Jude—Jude
Rev—Revelation

Nihil obstat: Robert C. Harren, J.C.L., *Censor deputatus.*

Imprimatur: ✚ George H. Speltz, D.D., Bishop of St. Cloud. July 22, 1982.

Printed in the United States of America.

Library of Congress Cataloging in Publication Data

Van Linden, Philip.
    The Gospel according to Mark.

    (Collegeville Bible commentary ; 2)
    Includes text of the Gospel of Mark.
    1. Bible. N.T. Mark—Commentaries. I. Bible.
N.T. Mark. English. New American. 1983. II. Title.
III. Series.
BS2585.2.V36   1983   226'.3077   82-20356
ISBN 0-8146-1302-0 (pbk.)

CONTENTS

Preface

It has been my experience over the years, and therefore it is my conviction, that the Gospel of Mark has its most profound effect on its readers when it is read *in one sitting*, from beginning to end (1:1–16:8). It is with this in mind that I invite those interested in Mark's Gospel to read it in its entirety before meditating on its individual parts. My brief introduction is meant to help today's Christians appreciate the overall drama and rhythm of the Gospel. Having seen the way Mark develops certain characters and themes as his drama progresses to its climax, his readers will be challenged to affirm in their own lives what it means to say that "Jesus is risen and alive in our midst!" That, after all, was Mark's purpose in gathering together the many scenes of Jesus' life and message in the first place. He wanted to involve his readers in a dynamic faith-encounter with the living, risen Lord.

Preparing this commentary on Mark's Gospel has been a spiritual experience for me. That did not come as a surprise, however, since it has happened before, to me and to other readers of his Gospel throughout the centuries. It is my hope that those who read Mark's drama today, as a whole and in its individual parts, will also experience much growth in their relationship with the risen Lord, alive in their midst!

PHILIP VAN LINDEN, C.M.
De Andreis Seminary
Lemont, Illinois

The Gospel According to Mark

Introduction

Mark's Gospel: one of four portraits of Jesus

It is commonly accepted by the majority of contemporary New Testament scholars that Mark's Gospel was the first to be written and that it was a source used by Matthew and Luke in the composition of their Gospels. (The Gospel of John, it seems, developed out of a tradition that did not know of the other three Gospels.) God's purpose in inspiring *four* evangelists was not primarily to "preserve the facts" about Jesus' life on earth but to meet the many different needs of the people in the newly formed first-century Christian community. God chose several believers to communicate the "good news" about Jesus in such a way that the various spiritual needs of the early church community could be met.

The Christian community today is also made up of people with a great variety of spiritual needs, and its faith can be nourished by the four inspired "Jesus portraits" of Mark, Matthew, Luke, and John. When Christians choose to encounter Mark's Jesus, they meet with that side of Jesus that is the simplest of the four, and very demanding! They discover that Mark's version of Jesus' life centers on his death and on the meaning of suffering. When they open themselves to involvement with Jesus as Mark presents him, they realize that they too are invited to discover the meaning of life and death as he did, namely, by radical trust in God and by loving service to others' needs.

A glimpse at the whole of Mark's Gospel

The overall plan and framework of Mark's Gospel is simple and involving. As his drama unfolds, his readers will be involved in the mystery of who Jesus is and what it means to be his follower. The Gospel develops gradually in three stages. In the *first stage* (chs. 1–8), Mark's readers are drawn into a relationship with the powerful healer and preacher, Jesus of Nazareth. During this first stage no one seems to understand Jesus' true identity, not even his disciples. Suddenly, in the encounter at Caesarea Philippi, what had been hinted at earlier (e.g., 3:6: "they took counsel . . . against him . . . to put him to death") becomes clear: "The Son of Man must suffer greatly . . . be killed, and rise after three days" (8:31). In this first climax of his

Gospel, Mark's readers also learn that the way of Christ is the way of the Christian (8:34: "Whoever wishes to come after me . . ."). Theirs too is the way of the cross!

The *second stage* of Mark's Gospel (chs. 9–15) gradually reveals to its readers the concrete means of true Christian discipleship. This is summed up best in 10:45, where Jesus says: "The Son of Man did not come to be served but to serve and to give his life as a ransom for many." And that is precisely what happens in the second climax of the Gospel, as Jesus dies for his people (chs. 14–15).

Jesus' death, however, is not the end. For the *third stage* of the Gospel of Mark begins with the proclamation of Jesus' resurrection and with his going to Galilee ahead of his disciples (16:6-7). It is at the empty tomb that Mark's readers take the place of Jesus' first followers and become the major characters in his Gospel drama (16:8). It is as his Gospel ends that Mark challenges his readers most dramatically to respond to Jesus in their lives with trust, and not with the trembling and bewilderment of the women at the tomb! The third stage of Mark's Gospel continues in the life of the church, until the risen Lord comes again.

The characters and themes in Mark's Gospel

Mark's narrative account of Jesus' ministry, death, and resurrection emphasizes certain themes that were of great importance in the early church. It is also important for the Christian community of the twentieth century to meditate upon them: (1) the *humanity* of Jesus; (2) *trust* as the heart of discipleship; and (3) *service to others* as the daily way of taking up Jesus' cup and cross.

1) Of the four Gospel portraits of Jesus, Mark's is by far the one that best reveals *the human side of Jesus*. While Mark's Jesus spends most of his time performing incredible acts of mercy, which reveal that he is God's Son, he is also depicted as a most human Lord. Only Mark preserves those details that bring out how sharp (1:25), deeply grieved and angry (3:5), or indignant (10:14) Jesus could be with those around him. Mark alone adds the touching detail to the story of Jesus' raising of the little girl from her deathbed: "she should be given something to eat" (5:43). Only Mark's Jesus looks at the rich man and *loves him* (10:21) before he challenges him to give up all to follow him. Mark's Jesus is often discouraged by his inability to get his own disciples to understand him and his mission (e.g., 4:13; 8:14-21). Mark reveals a Jesus who is at once the powerful Son of God and a most human person. Mark's readers will sense that the Jesus of this Gospel is very approachable, because he has experienced life as they have, with all its disappointments and its loves, with all its joy and sadness.

2) Mark believes that the truest sign of being Jesus' disciple is *trust*. He challenges his readers to a radical trust in the risen Lord in a most provocative way by portraying Jesus' first disciples as slow-witted, even blind. Mark's Jesus looks for *trust in who he is*, but the disciples respond with *amazement and fear to what he does*! They see who Jesus is on one level (their Messiah-Savior, who gives them bread, in 6:34-44 and 8:1-10). But they are blind to him on another level (their Messiah-Suffering Servant, who gives them life through his death, in 10:35-45). The Jesus who could give sight to the physically blind (8:22-26; 10:46-52) could not give insight and understanding to his most intimate followers!

The blindness of Jesus' disciples is one of the tragic threads of Mark's narrative. In presenting them in this way, however, Mark hopes that his Christian readers will *see* better than Jesus' first disciples did. He hopes that they will trust in Jesus, not as the "instant cure-all Messiah," but as the one whose death gives meaning to the life and suffering they experience.

3) A final cluster of Markan images is closely related to Mark's presentation of the human Jesus and the blind disciples. Jesus' challenge to trust in him leads to *the cup and the cross*. And in concrete daily life, Jesus' cup and cross take the form of being "the slave of all" and serving others rather than being served by them (10:44f.). Although Mark's Gospel does not give long lists of "how to" serve God and others, its readers cannot avoid the model of Mark's Jesus as the suffering servant of all. They know that they must seize every opportunity to serve others in charity if they want to be his followers.

It is in the garden of Gethsemane that the major themes of Mark's Gospel seem to come together. In his agony there, the human heart of Jesus is "troubled and distressed" (14:33). The one who has challenged his disciples to trust in God alone comes close to giving up himself: "Father . . . take this cup away from me." However, as his disciples sleep, Jesus continues his prayer in faith: "but not what I will but what you will" (14:36). Anyone searching for the meaning of Christian life and discipleship in Mark's Gospel can turn to the Gethsemane passage (14:32-42) and hear it all summed up: "Give yourself to the suffering Messiah. Trust as he did, even though he would rather not have trusted. Join him in serving the needs of your brothers and sisters, even unto death."

The Gospel of Mark in the liturgy

For centuries most of the readings at Sunday Eucharists were chosen from the Gospel according to Matthew. With the renewal of the liturgy after the Second Vatican Council, there came a major restructuring of the Gospels to be proclaimed on Sundays. Mark's Gospel became the "Cycle B Gospel," read on most Sundays from January to November every third year (1988, 1991, 1994, etc.). Weekday Eucharists feature Mark's Gospel even more regularly, daily during the eight weeks that precede the Lenten season. Consequently, by being open to the Liturgy of the Word, Christians can now experience the person and message of Mark's Gospel on a regular basis, in union with all those who share in the church's liturgy. With all of God's people, they are invited to follow Mark's Jesus from his baptism and first preaching (1:7-11 and 1:14-20: Third Sunday in Ordinary Time) to his last days before entering upon his passion (13:24-32: Thirty-third Sunday in Ordinary Time). The liturgical experience of Mark's Gospel can thus be very formative of the church's relationship with Jesus. It can also serve as a weekly, even daily, rallying call to deeper involvement in service to others, which is the hallmark of the Markan Christian.

The author and his times: A matter of urgency

According to some fathers of the early church (e.g., Papias, A.D. 135; Irenaeus, A.D. 200; and Origen, A.D. 250), the "Gospel according to Mark" was the work of an associate and interpreter of Peter. The Acts of the Apostles links a certain "John Mark" with Peter (Acts 12:12), and the First Letter of Peter concludes with encouragement from Peter and greetings from "Mark my son" (1 Pet 5:13). Most scholars today feel that the tradition of Peter's influence on Mark's Gospel was more practical than historical, that is, such a tradition assured this Gospel of apostolic authority ("It came to the church through Mark from Peter!"), which was so important in the formative years of the church. From the Gospel itself, it is possible only to identify its au-

---

Almost all of Jesus' activity in the first nine chapters of Mark's Gospel takes place in or around Galilee, in the north of Palestine. In chapters 10–16, which describe the last weeks of Jesus' preaching and teaching, everything happens in Judea and in Jerusalem, the place of his death and resurrection. Mark concludes his Gospel with the young man's message to the women at the empty tomb: "Go now and tell his disciples and Peter, 'He is going before you to Galilee; there you will see him as he told you'" (16:7, referring to 14:28).

Mark seems to use geography in a very symbolic way. By having Jesus spend so much time in Galilee, it is likely that Mark was symbolizing the mission of the early church, in the name of Jesus, to the Gentile world. The final promise of Jesus, then, to go before them to Galilee would mean two things to Mark's readers: (1) it will be in "Galilee," in the church's mission to the Gentiles, that they will see the risen Lord going ahead of them; (2) once the good news has been proclaimed to the Gentiles (13:10), Jesus will come again to gather "his elect from the four winds" (13:27).

PALESTINE IN THE
TIME OF JESUS

Miles
0   40

Kms
0   40

Sidon
Abila
ABILENE
Damascus
Zarephath
LEBANON MTS.
S Y R I A
MT. HERMON
Tyre
PHOENICIA
Caesarea Philippi
MEDITERRANEAN
GALILEE
Chorazin
Bethsaida
Ptolemais
Capernaum
Lake
SEA
Magadan
Cana
Tiberias
Galilee
MT. CARMEL
Nazareth
MT.
TABOR
Nain
Gadara
Caesarea
TEN TOWNS
Salim
SAMARIA
Aenon
Samaria
MT. EBAL
Gerasa
MT. GERIZIM
Sychar
Jordan River
P E R E A
Arimathea?
Joppa
Ephraim
Jericho
Bethany
Emmaus
Bethany
Azotus
Jerusalem
Qumran
Ascalon
J U D E A
Bethlehem
Gaza
Hebron
Dead
Sea
N A B A T E A
I D U M E A

© United Bible Societies, 1978

thor as a zealous member (pastor?) of the second-generation church, who seems to be writing around the time of the destruction of Jerusalem by the Roman army in A.D. 70 (see especially 13:1-23 for indications of this time-frame).

It also becomes evident as one reads Mark's Gospel that his message is a most urgent one. It seems that Mark and his community belonged to that part of the early Christian community which believed that Jesus was going to return very soon, *as he said* (9:1; 13:30-31). In order to be on guard and ready for his glorious return as "Son of Man coming in the clouds . . . to gather his elect" (13:26-27), Mark urges his Christians to learn from his Jesus the meaning of radical, here-and-now discipleship, as if there is no tomorrow.

And so it begins, "the gospel of Jesus Christ, the Son of God," according to Mark.

The Gospel According to Mark

Text and Commentary

I: THE PREPARATION FOR THE PUBLIC MINISTRY OF JESUS

1 ¹The beginning of the gospel of Jesus Christ [the Son of God].

The Preaching of John the Baptist. ²As it is written in Isaiah the prophet:
"Behold, I am sending my messenger ahead of you;
he will prepare your way.

³A voice of one crying out in the desert:
'Prepare the way of the Lord,
make straight his paths.'"

⁴John [the] Baptist appeared in the desert proclaiming a baptism of repentance for the forgiveness of sins. ⁵People of the whole Judean countryside and all the inhabitants of Jerusalem were going out to him and were being baptized by him in

"AND SO IT BEGINS"

Mark 1:1-45

The Gospel of Mark begins with a powerful title sentence. In his theme verse, Mark announces his belief that *Jesus of Nazareth*, who had lived among the people of Palestine for some thirty years, healing their sick and teaching them the goodness of God, and who had been put to death among thieves, *is indeed alive as the risen Christ, the Son of God.*

Mark, unlike Matthew and Luke, does not relate anything about the infancy of Jesus; instead, he immediately introduces his readers to the adult Jesus through his forerunner, John the Baptist. Mark's readers are quickly drawn into the drama of Jesus' active ministry. They witness Jesus' miraculous power and the ensuing conflicts with those who fail to understand his life's mission. The drama that begins here in chapter 1 will eventually unfold in the final mystery of conflict and power, the death and resurrection of Jesus. It is in the crucified and risen Jesus that Mark and his Christian readers find their source of hope and strength for living as Jesus did.

1:1 The Son of God. Mark's first verse is more power-packed than a casual reading would suggest. It is more than a title verse, announcing the Gospel's central character: Jesus Christ, the Son of God. It also provides the key to understanding the succeeding sixteen chapters. That is because in only one other place in the Gospel does a human being proclaim that Jesus is Son of God (the centurion who put Jesus to death, in 15:39). This prepares Mark's

the Jordan River as they acknowledged their sins. ⁶John was clothed in camel's hair, with a leather belt around his waist. He fed on locusts and wild honey. ⁷And this is what he proclaimed: "One mightier than I is coming after me. I am not worthy to stoop and loosen the thongs of his sandals. ⁸I have baptized you with water; he will baptize you with the holy Spirit."

The Baptism of Jesus. ⁹It happened in those days that Jesus came from Nazareth of Galilee and was baptized in the Jordan by John. ¹⁰On coming up out of the water he saw the heavens being torn open and the Spirit, like a dove, descending upon

readers to question their own faith-convictions about Jesus of Nazareth. According to Mark, no one else would recognize Jesus' true identity while living with him and witnessing his powerful teaching and healing. In his first verse, Mark gives his readers the clue to the end and purpose of his whole Gospel: to know Jesus as the Son of God is to believe that he is their suffering Messiah, who died on the cross and who now lives as their risen Lord. Mark's Jesus asks his disciples to follow him to life on his way—the way of loving service, even unto death.

1:2-8 John points to Jesus. John the Baptist has only one function in the Gospel of Mark: he is the one who points to Jesus as the Messiah. His call for conversion to God through baptism and the forgiveness of sins, as well as his clothes and food, makes him the new Elijah (see 2 Kgs 1:8) sent by God "to prepare the way of the Lord." John recognizes that one more powerful is soon to come after him. Although Jesus will be baptized by John, it is clear that even John knows his subordinate role in the Jesus drama. As Mark's narrative unfolds, he will present John the Baptist again, in 6:14-29. There, by his death at the hands of King Herod, John will fulfill the role of pointing to Jesus' death, just as here his baptism with water points to Jesus' baptism "with the Holy Spirit." John's whole courageous life and death point to Jesus of Nazareth. He is a model of total witness to Christ for Mark's readers.

1:9-11 God confirms John's preaching. What John's preaching points to, God himself confirms. Although Jesus comes from Nazareth to be baptized by John in the Jordan River (Matthew, Luke, and John diminish John's role in Jesus' baptism), Mark makes it very clear that it is God himself who blesses Jesus. It is God who rends the heavens, sends his Spirit upon Jesus in the form of a dove, and says: "You are my beloved Son. With you I am well pleased." God likewise has descended upon Christians in their baptism, making them favored sons and daughters of God. As Mark's readers follow *the* Son, they learn how to be like him. They see how he let the Spirit of his baptism lead him to drink the cup of suffering at the end of his life of service and interpret his impending death as a second "baptism" which his disciples would share (10:35-45).

him. ¹¹And a voice came from the heavens, "You are my beloved Son; with you I am well pleased."

The Temptation of Jesus. ¹²At once the Spirit drove him out into the desert, ¹³and he remained in the desert for forty days, tempted by Satan. He was among wild beasts, and the angels ministered to him.

II: THE MYSTERY OF JESUS

The Beginning of the Galilean Ministry. ¹⁴After John had been arrested, Jesus came to Galilee proclaiming the gospel of God: ¹⁵"This is the time of fulfillment. The kingdom of God is at hand. Repent, and believe in the gospel."

The Call of the First Disciples. ¹⁶As he passed by the Sea of Galilee, he saw Simon and his brother Andrew casting their nets into the sea; they were fishermen. ¹⁷Jesus said to them, "Come after me, and I will make you fishers of men." ¹⁸Then they left their nets and followed him. ¹⁹He walked along a little farther and saw

1:12-15 Jesus' journey begins. Mark's version of the temptation in the desert is much shorter than Matthew's or Luke's. Its brevity, however, makes its significance more direct. The Spirit leads Jesus into the desert. Tempted and tested there by Satan for forty days, as the people of Israel were tested before him, Jesus is protected by God through his angels. Mark's two verses state simply that Jesus has withstood the test and is ready for his brief but saving life of service to God and humanity. Experiences of temptation and weakness were not unknown to the Son of God. Mark thus tells his readers that the protecting spirit of Jesus is with them in their weakness just as God was with him in his desert experience.

With John's arrest (v. 14), Jesus' work begins. Mark's "gospel of Jesus Christ, the Son of God" began at verse 1. Now the "good news of God" begins, as Jesus' first words are heard: "This is the time of fulfillment" (v. 15). Yes, says Mark, God's reign of power has begun in Jesus, who is God's good news in person. Jesus' announcement would have exhilarated the faithful Israelites of his day. However, he immediately links the good news with an equally important call for radical response: "Therefore, repent and put all your trust in the gospel of God that I bear!" In these brief inaugural words of Jesus' ministry, Mark summarizes the gospel message that Jesus preached: the very power of God is available to those who open themselves to Jesus and to his gospel way of loving service.

1:16-20 The call of the first four followers. Jesus, who has just begun preaching about the kingdom of God and conversion, effects what he preaches. Immediately after Jesus says "Come after me" to the brothers Simon and Andrew, James and John, they turn from family and lifework as fishermen to follow him. In this brief but very striking scene, Mark shows how powerful and direct Jesus' call to share in his mission can be. He also holds up as a model for his readers the immediate and total response of the four. But if Mark's readers are to gain the full impact of this passage, it is vital

15

James, the son of Zebedee, and his brother John. They too were in a boat mending their nets. [20]Then he called them. So they left their father Zebedee in the boat along with the hired men and followed him.

The Cure of a Demoniac. [21]Then they came to Capernaum, and on the sabbath he entered the synagogue and taught. [22]The people were astonished at his teaching, for he taught them as one having authority and not as the scribes. [23]In their synagogue was a man with an unclean spirit; [24]he cried out, "What have you to do with us, Jesus of Nazareth? Have you come to destroy us? I know who you

that they be aware of how Simon (named Peter by Jesus in 3:16), James, and John will respond elsewhere in the Gospel. (Andrew is mentioned only three other times: when Simon's mother-in-law is cured, 1:29; when Jesus names him among the Twelve, 3:18; and when he is with Peter, James, and John again, talking with Jesus about the end of the temple, 13:3.)

This first involvement of Peter, James, and John with Jesus is only the beginning of an exciting yet tension-filled journey. These three will be the only ones whom Jesus permits to share in four experiences in which he most clearly reveals the power and purpose of his life (healing and giving life, in 1:29-31 and 5:37-43; the glory-filled transfiguration, in 9:2-13; the message about the future times, in 13:1-37). At the same time, they will be the ones who will most seriously misunderstand their Lord and fail him at crucial points of their intimacy with him (Peter at Caesarea Philippi, in 8:27-33; James and John seeking "to be first," in 10:35-45; all three of them in the garden of Gethsemane, in 14:32-42; Peter's denial, in 15:66-72).

The eager and total response of the disciples here, once seen in Mark's overall drama, draws the readers of the Gospel into a tension that will be experienced over and over as the journey with Jesus unfolds. For Mark, to "come after" Jesus and to join in his mission means to walk a journey of life-giving exhilaration and draining confusion, of overwhelming power and powerlessness. It is an invitation to respond, "Yes, I leave all and follow you," not only in one radical conversion experience but continuously until the end.

1:21-28 Spellbound and amazed by his teaching and power. Mark's readers do not learn *what* Jesus teaches in the Capernaum synagogue, but they do learn *how* he teaches ("with authority," vv. 22 and 27), and *what effect* his powerful teaching has (people are "astonished" and "amazed," vv. 22 and 27; the unclean spirit is overwhelmed, v. 26). The repetition of the phrase "with authority" (found twice, at v. 22 and v. 27) indicates that Mark wants the events of Jesus' first teaching and first powerful action to be seen as intimately related. He not only speaks with authority—he also acts with power!

It is important to know that for Mark and his first-century Christians the "unclean spirit" (v. 23) and other "demons" (see 1:32; 3:11, 15, 22; 5:2,

"Come after me; I will make you fishers of men" (Mark 1:17).

Shoreline of the Sea of Galilee

Ruins of the synagogue at Capernaum, probably built on the site of the synagogue in which Jesus taught (Mark 1:21).

Ruins of private houses in Capernaum, among which is located the house of Peter (Mark 1:29)

are—the Holy One of God!" 25Jesus rebuked him and said, "Quiet! Come out of him!" 26The unclean spirit convulsed him and with a loud cry came out of him. 27All were amazed and asked one another, "What is this? A new teaching with authority. He commands even the unclean spirits and they obey him." 28His fame spread everywhere throughout the whole region of Galilee.

The Cure of Simon's Mother-in-Law. 29On leaving the synagogue he entered the house of Simon and Andrew with James and John. 30Simon's mother-in-law lay sick with a fever. They immediately told him about her. 31He approached, grasped

etc.) represented evil, mysterious powers who were hostile to God, health, and goodness. These demons were thought to be so perceptive that they could know who was a representative of God's power. Here, the "unclean spirit" reveals Jesus as "the holy One of God" (v. 24) and cunningly tries to thwart his mission for goodness. Jesus' two commands are sharper and more forceful than the challenges of the unclean spirit. For *Jesus' word effects what it says:* the unclean spirit leaves the man, shrieking one last time as he goes down in defeat (v. 26). The "amazed" bystanders acknowledge the teacher's authority, yet they still have to ask: "What is this?" (v. 27).

Mark's intention here is to make his readers confident in their Lord as teacher and healer. However, the allusion to the people's amazement (v. 27), which caused Jesus' reputation to spread throughout Galilee (v. 28), also has another purpose. It is precisely the people's response of being *amazed* (1:27 and 5:20), or *astounded* (2:12 and 5:42) that will eventually bring other hostile forces to seek to destroy Jesus (see 6:14-29, where Herod is threatened by Jesus' reputation and ends up beheading John the Baptist). Mark wants more from his readers than amazement; he wants them to be alert when Jesus reveals himself in less appealing ways. "Will you also be amazed when Jesus begins to teach that the Son of Man has to suffer much, be rejected by the chief priests, be put to death, and rise three days later (8:31)? Will you recognize him for who he is when he hangs on the cross, abandoned by most of his followers who were amazed by his first signs of power?"

The followers of Mark's Jesus can have much confidence in Jesus as wonderworker. However, those who want to follow the "amazing one" must also go the way he goes. They must deny themselves, take up their cross, and follow after him (8:34).

1:29-31 Simon's mother-in-law. In verse 29, Mark has Jesus move immediately from his first powerful miracle to another. The visit to Simon's mother-in-law turns into a second sign that God's kingdom of wholeness is present in him. In 1:25 Jesus cured with a word; here he cures sickness by a touch (1:31). His touch saves as surely as his word. The fact that the woman's cure is immediate and total is made clear by Mark's emphasis on how she resumes her duties of hospitality, waiting on her guests in verse 31.

her hand, and helped her up. Then the fever left her and she waited on them.

Other Healings. ³²When it was evening, after sunset, they brought to him all who were ill or possessed by demons. ³³The whole town was gathered at the door. ³⁴He cured many who were sick with various diseases, and he drove out many demons, not permitting them to speak because they knew him.

Jesus Leaves Capernaum. ³⁵Rising very early before dawn, he left and went off to a deserted place, where he prayed. ³⁶Simon and those who were with him pursued him ³⁷and on finding him said, "Everyone is looking for you." ³⁸He told them, "Let us go on to the nearby villages that I may preach there also. For this purpose have I come." ³⁹So he went into their synagogues, preaching and driving out demons throughout the whole of Galilee.

The Cleansing of a Leper. ⁴⁰A leper came to him [and kneeling down] begged him and said, "If you wish, you can make me clean." ⁴¹Moved with pity, he stretched out his hand, touched him, and said to him, "I do will it. Be made clean." ⁴²The leprosy left him immediately, and

1:32-34 The Messiah and his secret. Jesus' first day of ministry does not end with sundown. That evening "the whole town" gathers around him with their sick and possessed. His first day of preaching and healing has given them hope that God is at work among them. After Jesus has cured many, Mark's readers first hear the curious phrase "not permitting them (the demons) to speak, because they knew him" (v. 34). This reminds Mark's readers of the "Quiet!" of 1:25 and prepares them for what they will hear repeatedly in Mark's Gospel (1:44; 3:12; 5:43; 7:36; 8:26; 8:30; 9:9). Mark presents Jesus as being very reserved about letting his reputation as miracle-worker spread. This reticence is called the "messianic secret." By emphasizing such secrecy regarding Jesus' identity as Messiah, Mark hopes that his Christian readers will accept Jesus' true identity, on his terms, in the context of his entire life and mission. Mark's Jesus will reveal himself as Messiah by being powerless on the cross. Christians are free to proclaim Jesus as their Messiah and Lord only when they accept his way of suffering messiahship along with his miraculous works.

1:35-39 The good news spreads. Jesus rises early and withdraws to a desert place to pray alone (v. 35), because he knows that the people are seeking him out *only* because of his miraculous powers. They have misunderstood him, and so he must move on to neighboring villages and continue his ministry of preaching and healing throughout all of Galilee (v. 39). Not even Simon can hold him back, for not even Simon understands where Jesus' way leads. Perhaps Mark's readers, who already know the end of the journey, will profit much from their own desert experiences of prayer with "the misunderstood Messiah."

1:40-45 The leper is healed and misunderstands. The healing of the leper is a remarkable scene, full of marked contrasts. It is a fitting conclusion to Mark's first chapter. The powerful but misunderstood Messiah is approached

he was made clean. ⁴³Then, warning him sternly, he dismissed him at once. ⁴⁴Then he said to him, "See that you tell no one anything, but go, show yourself to the priest and offer for your cleansing what Moses prescribed; that will be proof for them." ⁴⁵The man went away and began to publicize the whole matter. He spread the report abroad so that it was impos-sible for Jesus to enter a town openly. He remained outside in deserted places, and people kept coming to him from every-where.

2 The Healing of a Paralytic. ¹When Jesus returned to Capernaum after some days, it became known that he was at home. ²Many gathered together so that there was no longer room for them, not

directly by a person who is normally denied any contact with healthy people. This outcast's trust in Jesus is met by the pity and power of his touch and word. However, the leper's exhilaration at his cure is dampened by a stern repetition of Jesus' prohibitive messianic secret: "Tell no one anything!" (v. 44). (Only the priest is to know, because only his word can allow the outcast to re-enter the society from which his sickness has kept him.)

Instead of following Jesus' word, the cured man tells everyone! And Jesus' mission is thwarted as soon as it begins: "It was impossible for Jesus to enter a town openly" (v. 45). Through this concluding story of chapter 1, Mark asks all Christian followers to take Jesus at his word. He asks them to take Jesus seriously, as he is, at his pace on the journey, and in his time. To be a Christian is to respond to Jesus' word with fidelity, whether that word is "Be made clean" or "Tell no one anything!"

JESUS IN CONFLICT

Mark 2:1–3:6

In Mark's first chapter, Jesus' appearance as teacher and healer had drawn the sick, possessed, and needy to him "from everywhere" (1:45). Now, in this section of five closely related scenes (2:1–3:6), Jesus' activity on behalf of those in need will draw the scrutinizing attention and threatening ire of the scribes and Pharisees, who make their first appearance in the Gospel.

The Markan drama continues to portray a powerful Jesus, whose "teach-ing with authority" (1:27) still issues forth in miraculous cures of the sick. But now there is more. Now it becomes evident that Jesus' claims to forgive sins (2:5) and to be "lord of the sabbath" (2:28) are the cause of open con-flict with the religious leaders of his day.

As Mark's readers journey with Jesus from the cure of the paralytic (2:1-12) to the cure of the man with the withered hand (3:1-6), they will sense an increasing tension. They will be lifted up with joy by Jesus' powerful but gentle love of the needy and outcast. They will swell with pride at their Lord's

even around the door, and he preached the word to them. ³They came bringing to him a paralytic carried by four men. ⁴Unable to get near Jesus because of the crowd, they opened up the roof above him. After they had broken through, they let down the mat on which the paralytic was lying. ⁵When Jesus saw their faith, he said to the paralytic, "Child, your sins are forgiven." ⁶Now some of the scribes were sitting there asking themselves, ⁷"Why does this man speak that way? He is blaspheming. Who but God alone can forgive sins?" ⁸Jesus immediately knew in his mind what they were thinking to themselves, so he said, "Why are you thinking such things in your hearts? ⁹Which is easier, to say to the paralytic, 'Your sins are forgiven,' or to say, 'Rise, pick up your mat and walk'? ¹⁰But that you may know that the Son of Man has authority to forgive sins on earth"—¹¹he said to the paralytic, "I say to you, rise, pick up your mat, and go home." ¹²He rose, picked up his mat at once, and went away in the sight of everyone. They were

wise teaching, which will eventually bring his wise antagonists to silence (3:4). At the same time, they will sense the dark place where all these "successful encounters" lead. They will sense that the Son of Man already stands in the shadow of the cross, even before Mark makes it clear at 3:6, when he concludes this section: "The Pharisees went out and immediately took counsel with the Herodians against him to put him to death." How well Mark prepares his Christian followers for the ultimate conflict of Jesus' life!

2:1-12 "My son, you are forgiven/healed." Back in Capernaum, Jesus is surrounded by great numbers of people again (v. 2; see 1:33). As he preaches to the crowd, four friends of a paralyzed man lower him on his mat through the roof so that he can be close enough for Jesus to see him and cure him (vv. 3-4). (Such extraordinary means to get close to Jesus emphasized the faith of these friends as well as the overwhelming size of the crowd Jesus attracted.) Jesus responds to this act of faith, not by healing the man immediately, but by touching off the first of a series of controversial dialogues with the onlooking scribes and Pharisees. When Jesus says, "Child, your sins are forgiven" (v. 5), he is as much as saying, "It is God whom you approach." (In the Old Testament, only God is capable of forgiving sins; and it was expected that he would do so only at the end of time.) It thus becomes clear why the scribes murmur "he is blaspheming" (v. 7) and why Jesus brings it all out in the open. His claim to be able to forgive sins better reveals his identity as Son of God than do the miracles he performs.

Aware of the silent censure his forgiving word has caused in the crowd, Jesus proceeds to prove that "the Son of Man has authority to forgive sins on earth" by commanding the man to rise and walk in the sight of everyone (vv. 8-11). In concluding this miracle, Mark asks his readers to praise God for his presence in their midst as the forgiver-healer, just as the crowd did (v. 12), even in the face of those who do not believe.

all astounded and glorified God, saying, "We have never seen anything like this."

The Call of Levi. ¹³Once again he went out along the sea. All the crowd came to him and he taught them. ¹⁴As he passed by, he saw Levi, son of Alphaeus, sitting at the customs post. He said to him, "Follow me." And he got up and followed him. ¹⁵While he was at table in his house, many tax collectors and sinners sat with Jesus and his disciples; for there were many who followed him. ¹⁶Some scribes who were Pharisees saw that he was eating with sinners and tax collectors and said to his disciples, "Why does he eat with tax collectors and sinners?" ¹⁷Jesus heard this and said to them [that], "Those who are well do not need a physician, but the sick do. I did not come to call the righteous but sinners."

The Question about Fasting. ¹⁸The disciples of John and of the Pharisees were

It is significant that Mark has chosen to present this miracle and teaching about Jesus' power to forgive sins so early in his Gospel drama. It shows that the need for the experience of God's forgiveness was as important to first-century Christians as it is today. Mark's readers praise God for saying clearly, even today, "My sons, my daughters, I absolve you from your sins."

2:13-22 Jesus and Levi; eating and fasting. After the conflict with the Pharisees over his dealing with the paralytic, Jesus continues to teach the crowds and to gather his first band of disciples (v. 13). He calls a tax collector, Levi, who immediately leaves his work to follow him (v. 14). It is significant that Jesus chooses his followers from among those with simple or even despicable occupations (for example, Levi would be held in contempt by his fellow Jews because he cooperated with the Romans in exacting taxes for the emperor. His profession would place him among the recognized sinners of the Jewish people).

Even more significant is the fact that Jesus goes to Levi's house to associate with other "sinners" (v. 15). This provokes the scribes, who object, "Why does he eat with tax collectors and sinners?" (v. 16). This Jewish teacher, in contrast to the Pharisees, seeks out sinners to follow him. He even eats with them! The entire scene ends with a general statement from Jesus: "Those who are well do not need a physician, but the sick do" (v. 17).

By relating this second conflict situation, Mark encourages his readers to understand that to follow Jesus means that their meals, especially their Eucharistic meals, must include people who are aware of their weakness and of their need of healing. This stands in contrast to anyone who might think that only those who are "righteous" may participate in the meal. Indeed, the meal at which Jesus is present as *the* righteous one is the meal at which the sick and the sinner are most welcome. Paradoxically, then, the Christian Eucharist is for those who seem "not to belong," but really do!

If Jesus' eating habits challenged the life style of the Jewish leaders, so also did his disciples' style of fasting (vv. 18-22). When confronted by the

accustomed to fast. People came to him and objected, "Why do the disciples of John and the disciples of the Pharisees fast, but your disciples do not fast?" [19]Jesus answered them, "Can the wedding guests fast while the bridegroom is with them? As long as they have the bridegroom with them they cannot fast. [20]But the days will come when the bridegroom is taken away from them, and then they will fast on that day. [21]No one sews a piece of unshrunken cloth on an old cloak. If he does, its fullness pulls away, the new from the old, and the tear gets worse. [22]Likewise, no one pours new wine into old wineskins. Otherwise, the wine will burst the skins, and both the wine and the skins are ruined. Rather, new wine is poured into fresh wineskins."

The Disciples and the Sabbath. [23]As he was passing through a field of grain on the sabbath, his disciples began to question why his disciples do not fast (v. 18), Jesus responds with his own question: "Why fast while the groom is at the wedding?" Drawing on Old Testament imagery (wedding imagery often referred to God's presence with his people, and fasting was seen as preparation for God's coming), Mark's Jesus is as much as saying that God's kingdom is now present in his person. Indeed, he goes on, once the groom is "taken away" (a reference to his death), the guests will fast until he returns in his glory (v. 20). As Mark's readers await that final coming of Jesus, they fast with a certain hope and joy in him.

Mark's readers today can live with the same joyful hope that Mark held out for his first readers. They too can understand the meaning of the two parables (the unshrunken cloth sewn on an old cloak, v. 21; and the new wine in old wineskins, v. 22), which are meant to teach that a true follower of Jesus does not fast for the wrong reasons. The kingdom of God has already been established. When Christians choose to fast, Mark implies, it is to heighten their anticipation of the full joy of the heavenly banquet they will share in. At the Eucharist, Christians already celebrate the groom's presence with them in sacrament. When they fast, they proclaim their hope in the fullness of union with him to come.

2:23-28 The lord of the sabbath. Mark next relates a peculiar incident about Jesus' disciples picking grain as they walk along with him on a sabbath. Again, the actions of Jesus and his followers cause a furor among the Pharisees. In response to their protest, Jesus argues from Scripture that even David took exception to the law for the sake of his hungry followers (1 Sam 21:2-7). Mark's Jesus goes on to proclaim that God created the sabbath for human beings, and not vice versa. Those who follow Jesus are to interpret the whole Jewish law by living according to God's spirit of the law, namely, loving kindness. Later in his Gospel, Mark will make it clear that all laws are summed up in the one law of Christ, his dual commandment of love. When a Christian chooses "to love God and one's neighbor as oneself," that one will be approved by the Lord (12:28-34).

make a path while picking the heads of grain. ²⁴ At this the Pharisees said to him, "Look, why are they doing what is unlawful on the sabbath?" ²⁵He said to them, "Have you never read what David did when he was in need and he and his companions were hungry? ²⁶How he went into the house of God when Abiathar was high priest and ate the bread of offering that only the priests could lawfully eat, and shared it with his companions?" ²⁷Then he said to them, "The sabbath was made for man, not man for the sabbath.

²⁸That is why the Son of Man is lord even of the sabbath."

3 A Man with a Withered Hand. ¹Again he entered the synagogue. There was a man there who had a withered hand. ²They watched him closely to see if he would cure him on the sabbath so that they might accuse him. ³He said to the man with the withered hand, "Come up here before us." ⁴Then he said to them, "Is it lawful to do good on the sabbath rather than to do evil, to save life rather than to destroy it?" But

The importance of this sabbath incident in Mark's Gospel lies in the summary character of its last verse. When Jesus says that the "Son of Man is lord even of the sabbath," he is summing up his own authority. Mark's readers will remember that this entire section began with Jesus' telling the crowd at Capernaum that "the Son of Man has authority to forgive sins on earth" (2:10). What happens next, on the same sabbath (3:1-6), will show how this claim of Mark's Jesus channels the flow of the whole Gospel. The Pharisees will stop arguing and begin plotting against the Son of Man. The die is cast!

(A note on the title "Son of Man": Jesus never refers to himself as the Son of God in Mark's Gospel. He often calls himself the Son of Man. This title, from Dan 7:13, came to be understood as referring to the future redeemer of the Israelite nation. Mark's use of the "Son of Man" title points rather to *the means* that the Redeemer would use to save his people, namely, his suffering and death on the cross. Mark's intention becomes even clearer when the reader notes that the next time the "Son of Man" title is used is in 8:31, in the first explicit prediction of Jesus' suffering and death.)

3:1-6 The withered hand and the plot. Jesus' mercy toward the man with the withered hand is the climax of the section that began with Jesus' cure of the paralyzed man (2:1-12). Its climactic nature becomes evident when one notices three things. First, Mark places this synagogue cure on the sabbath, immediately after the statement that Jesus is lord of the sabbath. The cure is concrete proof of his claim to lordship. Secondly, a dramatic change of rhythm in the narrative becomes evident when one reads the withered-hand passage in connection with the four preceding ones. Here it is Jesus who asks the provocative question ("Is it lawful to do good on the sabbath . . . ?," v. 4), not the Pharisees, as they do in 2:7, 16, 18, 24. Here Jesus is angry with them (v. 5), instead of them being upset with him. In fact, now the complainers have nothing to say (v. 5)! Thirdly, after Jesus

they remained silent. ⁵Looking around at them with anger and grieved at their hardness of heart, he said to the man, "Stretch out your hand." He stretched it out and his hand was restored. ⁶The Pharisees went out and immediately took counsel with the Herodians against him to put him to death.

The Mercy of Jesus. ⁷Jesus withdrew toward the sea with his disciples. A large number of people [followed] from Galilee and from Judea. ⁸Hearing what he was doing, a large number of people came to him also from Jerusalem, from Idumea, from beyond the Jordan, and from the neighborhood of Tyre and Sidon. ⁹He told his disciples to have a boat ready for him because of the crowd, so that they would not crush him. ¹⁰He had cured many and, as a result, those who had dis-

shows his merciful power by perfectly restoring the man's hand, the Pharisees withdraw to plot how they might destroy Jesus (v. 6).

Mark concludes this series of five "conflict stories" on a sobering note. His readers cannot help but see that Jesus' way of life is leading to his death (v. 6). They also realize that Mark will suggest that the same is true for those who follow the "Son of Man" (8:31-38). Nevertheless, no matter what tension Mark's readers will experience while trying to live the Christian life, Jesus will be there on their behalf. Mark has assured his readers that Jesus will respond generously to their faith in him (2:5), because he has come for the needy (2:17) as a merciful Lord of the sabbath (2:27 and 3:4-5).

REFLECTING ON THE MEANING OF DISCIPLESHIP

Mark 3:7-35

Good storytellers involve their listeners in their stories by the use of various techniques, such as character development, comparison and contrast, vivid detail, pacing, etc. In his first two chapters Mark has already shown that he is a good storyteller. He has begun to reveal the human side of Jesus' character by certain details that Matthew and Luke leave out of their accounts (for example, only Mark describes Jesus' grief and anger during the cure of the man with the withered hand, 3:5). He has already established a mounting tension in his drama by placing the five conflict stories of 2:1–3:6 (they "took counsel against him to put him to death," 3:6) after the "success story" of chapter 1 ("people kept coming to him from everywhere!" 1:45).

Mark the storyteller also has a message he wants to convey by his Jesus story, and so he wants to give his readers time for reflection. That is why he presents a brief summary passage here (3:7-12). It not only sums up Jesus' overwhelming appeal to the crowds (vv. 7-10), but it also reminds his read-

eases were pressing upon him to touch him. [11]And whenever unclean spirits saw him they would fall down before him and shout, "You are the Son of God." [12]He warned them sternly not to make him known.

The Mission of the Twelve. [13]He went up the mountain and summoned those whom he wanted and they came to him. [14]He appointed twelve [whom he also named apostles] that they might be with him and he might send them forth to preach [15]and to have authority to drive out demons: [16][he appointed the twelve:] Simon, whom he named Peter; [17]James, son of Zebedee, and John the brother of

ers that Jesus did not want his identity as God's Son to be proclaimed for the wrong reasons (vv. 11-12; see the comment on "secret" in 1:32-34). Mark hopes that this pause for reflection will prepare his readers for the rest of their journey with Jesus. Their walk with him will often be confused by "great crowds and multitudes" in search of only a part of what Jesus and Christians come to give (vv. 7-8). It will be complicated by forces bent on obstructing the path that leads to the fulfillment of the Lord's mission (vv. 11-12). Therefore, Mark rounds off this part of his Jesus story with two passages (the choice of the Twelve, vv. 13-19, and the conflict about Beelzebul, vv. 20-35) which help his readers to understand the true meaning of Christian discipleship.

3:13-19 Called by name to be with Jesus. By the time Mark wrote his Gospel in A.D. 70, most of those who had been Jesus' first disciples were no longer present to lead the Christian community. In this passage, in which Jesus' choice of the first twelve disciples is described, Mark emphasizes for the Christians of his day two important elements of discipleship: "being with Jesus" and "being named" by him.

The first ingredient of Christian discipleship emphasized here is being a "companion" of the Lord (v. 14). To be Jesus' "disciple" is to be a "learner," and to learn from him it is necessary to be with him. From this point on in the Gospel narrative, Jesus will keep his Twelve close to him. They will learn from him the mysteries of the kingdom (in parables, 4:1-34). They will also discover the difficulties of his way (chs. 8–16, in which Jesus details his way of the cross and the cost of following him). The fact that Mark has Jesus choose his Twelve on the mountain (v. 13) not only indicates the solemnity of the moment but also points to other scenes of the Gospel when the disciples will be with Jesus on other mountaintops, for example, to witness the transfiguration in 9:2-10 and to see him in agony on the Mount of Olives in 14:26-42. Mark's readers are asked to be with Jesus and to learn from him in experiences of mysterious glory and painful agony.

A second element of Christian discipleship is located in the meaning of "being named" by Jesus. In Genesis, because God had "named" the heavens

James, whom he named Boanerges, that is, sons of thunder; ¹⁸Andrew, Philip, Bartholomew, Matthew, Thomas, James the son of Alphaeus; Thaddeus, Simon the Cananean, ¹⁹and Judas Iscariot who betrayed him.

Blasphemy of the Scribes. ²⁰He came home. Again [the] crowd gathered, making it impossible for them even to eat. ²¹When his relatives heard of this they set out to seize him, for they said, "He is out of his mind." ²²The scribes who had come from Jerusalem said, "He is possessed by Beelzebul," and "By the prince of demons he drives out demons."

Jesus and Beelzebul. ²³Summoning them, he began to speak to them in parables, "How can Satan drive out Satan? ²⁴If a kingdom is divided against itself, that kingdom cannot stand. ²⁵And if a house is divided against itself, that house will not be able to stand. ²⁶And if Satan has risen up against himself and is divided, he cannot stand; that is the end of him. ²⁷But no one can enter a strong man's house to plunder his property un-

and the earth and all creatures, they became God's own possession (Gen 1:3-10). When God gave Adam the command to name the animals, Adam shared God's own power over them (Gen 2:20). To be "named" by Jesus means to be possessed by him, to be under his control. It also means that those named by him will share in his power (vv. 14-15). In this brief passage, Mark's readers, baptized "in the name of Jesus," hear the invitation to be companions with the risen Lord and to learn from him how to share in his mission and power.

3:20-35 Possessed by God and doing God's will. Once Jesus has come down from the mountain with his twelve companions, many people crowd around him, so much so that he and his disciples cannot even manage to eat (v. 20). Mark's readers will notice various reactions to Jesus and to his ministry among the people. His family is "standing outside." They have come to protect him from doing too much. They think he is "out of his mind" (v. 21). Important scribes have come from Jerusalem to see why Jesus is so popular. They claim that he is "possessed by Beelzebul" and that he expels demons with Satan's help (v. 22). After Jesus has cleverly and forcefully responded to these accusations (vv. 23-30), Mark's readers learn what the proper reaction to Jesus is. They learn that, of all those who crowd around Jesus, the only ones who can really be considered his brothers and sisters are those "who do the will of God" (vv. 32-34). Jesus expects his followers to have the same single-minded dedication to God's will as he does. Such dedication may lead to conflicts with people like the Jerusalem scribes. It may seem "crazy" or "overdone" to others, even to members of one's own family! But this is what it means to be "family" with Jesus.

Jesus' response to the accusation that he is possessed by the devil is brief and pointed. In two parables about divided kingdoms and divided houses (vv. 24-27), he shows how self-defeating it would be if he, who drives evil

less he first ties up the strong man. Then he can plunder his house. ²⁸Amen, I say to you, all sins and all blasphemies that people utter will be forgiven them. ²⁹But whoever blasphemes against the holy Spirit will never have forgiveness, but is guilty of an everlasting sin." ³⁰For they had said, "He has an unclean spirit."

Jesus and His Family. ³¹His mother and his brothers arrived. Standing outside they sent word to him and called him. ³²A crowd seated around him told him, "Your mother and your brothers [and your sisters] are outside asking for you." ³³But he said to them in reply, "Who are my mother and [my] brothers?" ³⁴And looking around at those seated in the circle he said, "Here are my mother and my brothers. ³⁵[For] whoever does the will of God is my brother and sister and mother."

4 **The Parable of the Sower.** ¹On another occasion he began to teach by the sea. A very large crowd gathered around him so that he got into a boat on the sea and sat down. And the whole crowd was beside the sea on land. ²And he taught them at length in parables, and in the course of his instruction he said to them, ³"Hear this! A sower went out to

spirits out of people (3:11), were an agent of Satan! Jesus also points out that the only unforgivable sin belongs to his accusers, who refuse to accept the power of God's Holy Spirit at work in him (vv. 28-30). Jesus is possessed by *God's* spirit, and so are all those who choose to do God's will.

THE MYSTERY OF THE KINGDOM; THE POWER OF JESUS

Mark 4:1-35

Chapter 4 begins and ends with Jesus in a boat. Mark's readers will hear him teaching the crowds "in parables" about the kingdom of God. This preaching will be followed by Jesus' revelation of his power over the raging sea. Jesus not only preaches about the power of the kingdom, but he also practices what he preaches!

4:1-20 Teaching in parables. C. H. Dodd, a renowned British Scripture scholar, describes what a parable is and how it was meant to function in the time of Jesus. "At its simplest, the parable is a metaphor or simile drawn from nature or common life, arresting the hearer by its vividness or strangeness, and leaving the mind in sufficient doubt about its precise application to tease it into active thought." Here in chapter 4, Mark puts his readers in touch with the first-century world of parables. They will hear how Jesus used the familiar in a new way, inviting his listeners to new thought about God and God's kingdom. In effect, Jesus' parables say that God's ways may not be our ways. They call for conversion.

In Jesus' first parable (vv. 3-8), Mark's readers hear that something small, like a seed (or like the small Christian community of A.D. 70), could grow

sow. ⁴And as he sowed, some seed fell on the path, and the birds came and ate it up. ⁵Other seed fell on rocky ground where it had little soil. It sprang up at once because the soil was not deep. ⁶And when the sun rose, it was scorched and it withered for lack of roots. ⁷Some seed fell among thorns, and the thorns grew up and choked it and it produced no grain. ⁸And some seed fell on rich soil and produced fruit. It came up and grew and yielded thirty, sixty, and a hundredfold." ⁹He added, "Whoever has ears to hear ought to hear."

The Purpose of the Parables. ¹⁰And when he was alone, those present along with the Twelve questioned him about the parables. ¹¹He answered them, "The mystery of the kingdom of God has been granted to you. But to those outside everything comes in parables, ¹²so that

'they may look and see but not perceive,
and hear and listen but not understand,
in order that they may not be converted and be forgiven.'"

¹³Jesus said to them, "Do you not understand this parable? Then how will you understand any of the parables? ¹⁴The sower sows the word. ¹⁵These are the ones on the path where the word is sown. As soon as they hear, Satan comes at once and

(or not grow) and yield (or not yield) much grain, depending on whether the soil was good (or thorny or rocky or hardened like the footpath). A good parable, by its nature, is open-ended and gives the hearer the choice to respond on various levels. Mark's hope in relating this parable is that his Christians would respond: "Let *us* be good soil! Let *us* be full of hope, even in the fragile times of our beginnings as a small community! *We* want God's seed to produce one hundredfold *in us*, as Jesus promised it would!"

The private discussion between Jesus and his disciples (vv. 10-12) sounds as though Jesus is giving the crowd ("those outside," v. 11) no chance to understand him or become his followers. This is very strange, considering that parables were meant to stimulate their hearers to conversion. What is going on in the harsh verse 12 (taken from Isa 6:9-10) is this: The early church knew that certain people had heard Jesus' word and had rejected him; they also knew that others ("you" disciples, in v. 11) had believed in him. Mark therefore shows that Jesus, like Isaiah before him, brought a message that truly caused people to take a stance, either for him or against him. Jesus' parables, says Mark, were intended to bring all people to God's kingdom, but some chose to remain "outside." Mark's readers are asked to be open to God's word in their day. They are challenged to let his word draw them "inside," into a deeper faith-relationship with their risen Lord.

Although Jesus' first parable was originally an open-ended invitation to radical involvement with him, the explanation that follows it (in vv. 13-20) becomes a practical, point-by-point application of the parable's details to the life of Mark's Christians. Listening carefully to this explanation, they could respond: "Yes, we understand the parable for our time (v. 13). We know

takes away the word sown in them. ¹⁶And these are the ones sown on rocky ground who, when they hear the word, receive it at once with joy. ¹⁷But they have no root; they last only for a time. Then when tribulation or persecution comes because of the word, they quickly fall away. ¹⁸Those sown among thorns are another sort. They are the people who hear the word, ¹⁹but worldly anxiety, the lure of riches, and the craving for other things intrude and choke the word, and it bears no fruit. ²⁰But those sown on rich soil are the ones who hear the word and accept it and bear fruit thirty and sixty and a hundredfold."

Parable of the Lamp. ²¹He said to them, "Is a lamp brought in to be placed under a bushel basket or under a bed, and not to be placed on a lampstand? ²²For there is nothing hidden except to be made visible; nothing is secret except to come to light. ²³Anyone who has ears to hear ought to hear." ²⁴He also told them, "Take care what you hear. The measure with which you measure will be measured out to you, and still more will be given to you. ²⁵To the one who has, more will be given; from the one who has not, even what he has will be taken away."

Seed Grows of Itself. ²⁶He said, "This is how it is with the kingdom of God; it is as if a man were to scatter seed on the land ²⁷and would sleep and rise night and day and the seed would sprout and grow, he knows not how. ²⁸Of its own accord the land yields fruit, first the blade, then the ear, then the full grain in the ear. ²⁹And when the grain is ripe, he wields the sickle at once, for the harvest has come."

The Mustard Seed. ³⁰He said, "To what shall we compare the kingdom of God, or what parable can we use for it? ³¹It is

that the seed is God's word (v. 14). But we also can see how the various types of seed stand for those people who respond to the word differently (vv. 13-20). Some of us have let Satan lead us away from the faith (v. 15). Some of our number let pressure and persecution wear us down (vv. 16-17). Others of us are struggling with cravings for money and other things of this world that draw us away (vv. 18-19). Nevertheless, we want to hear the word, take it to heart, and be true followers of Jesus' way" (v. 20).

4:21-34 Hearing the word in parables. After the parable of the seed and its explanation, Mark records five other parables that are meant to enable his audience to take Jesus' word to heart more personally and more profoundly. By the parable of the lamp (v. 21), Mark suggests that his readers will have to ponder the meaning of Jesus' life and message much more thoroughly for themselves before they can share it fully with others (vv. 22-23). The parable-like saying about getting back "in the measure you give" (v. 24) is much like the preceding parable about the lamp. Mark's readers must continuously grow in their understanding of Jesus for themselves, or they will lose what they think they possess. The parable of the sleeping farmer (vv. 26-29) shatters the illusions of those who think that they can control the coming of God's kingdom. Indeed, says Mark, "God's ways are not our ways! We must be patient and let God be God!" The last parable of chapter

like a mustard seed that, when it is sown in the ground, is the smallest of all the seeds on the earth. ³²But once it is sown, it springs up and becomes the largest of plants and puts forth large branches, so that the birds of the sky can dwell in its shade." ³³With many such parables he spoke the word to them as they were able to understand it. ³⁴Without parables he did not speak to them, but to his own disciples he explained everything in private.

The Calming of a Storm at Sea. ³⁵On that day, as evening drew on, he said to them, "Let us cross to the other side." ³⁶Leaving the crowd, they took him with them in the boat just as he was. And other boats were with him. ³⁷A violent squall came up and waves were breaking over the boat, so that it was already filling up. ³⁸Jesus was in the stern, asleep on a cushion. They woke him and said to him, "Teacher, do you not care that we are perishing?" ³⁹He woke up, rebuked the wind, and said to the sea, "Quiet! Be still!" The wind ceased and there was great calm. ⁴⁰Then he asked them, "Why are you terrified? Do you not yet have faith?" ⁴¹They were filled with great awe and said to one another, "Who then is this whom even wind and sea obey?"

4 is also about a seed, the smallest of all seeds, the mustard seed (vv. 30-32). Even though the early Christian community was small in number, this parable assures Mark's readers that all their efforts will be fruitful in the growing kingdom of God—if they will just understand (see vv. 33-34).

Mark summarizes how the people "heard" Jesus' parables: some attentive ones "were able to understand" them (v. 33), while the disciples understood them perfectly because "he explained everything in private" to them (v. 34). With such special tutoring, Jesus' disciples would seem ready to prove their enlightened discipleship. The following scene on the sea is proof that they were *not* ready!

4:35-41 Jesus stills the storm and calls for faith. In this first storm scene (see 6:45-52 for a similar account), Mark's Jesus gives his disciples an opportunity to show that they have come to know him for who he really is. They have shared in the secrets of the kingdom (4:1-34), and they have been with him as he healed all sickness and drove out demons (chs. 1-3). Now they are with him on the raging sea, and he sleeps! (v. 38). They think that he does not care for them (v. 38), after all they have seen him do on behalf of those in need. After quieting the violent storm with a word, "Quiet! Be still!" (v. 39), Jesus turns to his disciples (and Mark's readers) and asks: "Why are you so terrified? Do you not yet have faith?" (v. 40). The first disciples' only response is: "Who then is this?" (v. 41). Mark wants his Christians, with their knowledge of Jesus' entire life, death, and resurrection, to be assured of his protection in their times of stress and confusion. He asks for more than "great awe" (v. 41) at Jesus' stilling of the storm. He asks for deep here-and-now faith from all who struggle to understand the meaning of Jesus' life, death, and resurrection in their own daily experience of Christian living.

5 **The Healing of the Gerasene Demoniac.** ¹They came to the other side of the sea, to the territory of the Gerasenes. ²When he got out of the boat, at once a man from the tombs who had an unclean spirit met him. ³The man had been dwelling among the tombs, and no one could restrain him any longer, even with a chain. ⁴In fact, he had frequently been bound with shackles and chains, but the chains had been pulled apart by him and the shackles smashed, and no one was strong enough to subdue him. ⁵Night and day among the tombs and on the hillsides he was always crying out and bruising himself with stones. ⁶Catching sight of Jesus from a distance, he ran up and prostrated himself before him, ⁷crying out in a loud voice, "What have you to do with me, Jesus, Son of the Most High God? I adjure you by God, do not torment me!" ⁸(He had been saying to him, "Unclean spirit, come out of the man!") ⁹He asked him, "What is your name?" He replied, "Legion is my name. There are many of us." ¹⁰And he pleaded earnestly with him not to drive them away from that territory.

¹¹Now a large herd of swine was feeding there on the hillside. ¹²And they pleaded with him, "Send us into the swine. Let us enter them." ¹³And he let them, and the unclean spirits came out and entered the swine. The herd of about

THE MIRACLES GO ON

Mark 5:1-43

The disciples, the Jewish leaders, and the Jewish crowds have all seen Jesus calm devils and the sea. They have heard him preach about conversion and the kingdom of God. After all this, the disciples still ask, "Who then is this?" (4:41). With the first miracle of chapter 5, Mark has Jesus reach out beyond Jewish boundaries to see if non-Jews will recognize him for who he really is (in 5:1-20, the cure of the demon-crazed man takes place in Gerasene-Gentile territory, east of the Jordan River). When Jesus returns home from this amazing encounter with non-Jews, he meets with increasingly more profound faith in him (from a Jewish synagogue official, Jairus, in 5:21-24 and 35-43, and from a simple, suffering woman in the crowd, in 5:25-34). It would seem that after these three miraculous events Jesus' disciples would understand his purpose and mission better. However, because the chapter ends with yet another reference to "the secret" ("He gave strict orders that no one should know this," 5:43), Mark's readers realize that Jesus still wants his followers to see more in him than a powerful worker of miracles.

5:1-20 Jesus reaches out to non-Jews: The Gerasene demoniac. Mark's vivid description of the possessed man, who violently roars around the tombs and hillsides of Gerasene territory (vv. 1-5), sets the stage for Jesus' encounter with him (vv. 6-10). Even before Jesus drives the devils from the man (strangely, the devils within the man *ask* Jesus to send them into a herd of swine, which he does, vv. 11-13), the possessed man comes to Jesus, pays

two thousand rushed down a steep bank into the sea, where they were drowned. [14]The swineherds ran away and reported the incident in the town and throughout the countryside. And people came out to see what had happened. [15]As they approached Jesus, they caught sight of the man who had been possessed by Legion, sitting there clothed and in his right mind. And they were seized with fear. [16]Those who witnessed the incident explained to them what had happened to the possessed man and to the swine. [17]Then they began

to beg him to leave their district. [18]As he was getting into the boat, the man who had been possessed pleaded to remain with him. [19]But he would not permit him but told him instead, "Go home to your family and announce to them all that the Lord in his pity has done for you." [20]Then the man went off and began to proclaim in the Decapolis what Jesus had done for him; and all were amazed.

Jairus's Daughter and the Woman with a Hemorrhage. [21]When Jesus had crossed again [in the boat] to the other

him the homage due to God alone, and recognizes him as God's Son (vv. 6-7). Like other possessed persons before him (see 1:24; 1:34; and 3:11), this man sees and proclaims what the disciples and the Jewish crowds do not: Jesus is God's Son!

When the people of the village come out to see if the swineherds' incredible story is true, they find their well-known wild man "sitting there clothed and in his right mind" (vv. 14-15). They also presumably see two thousand pigs afloat in the sea. Naturally, they are filled with fear. They cannot fathom the power of Jesus and ask him to leave their land before he shocks them any more. It was obviously easier for them to cope with a violent possessed man than it was to deal with the one who had the power to cure him (vv. 16-17). The healed man, so long tormented and isolated from society, asks if he can stay with Jesus (v. 18). Although Jesus does not let him come along with him, he does not tell him to keep quiet about the cure, as he has so often done after his miracles. The consequence is that the non-Jews throughout the region of the Ten Cities hear what God's mercy has done for him through Jesus (vv. 19-20). By this remarkable miracle, Mark not only displays Jesus' loving concern for one outcast but also sets the stage for Jesus' mission to all non-Jews.

Mark's community of Jewish *and* Gentile Christians would be very alert as Jesus enters the foreign land of Gerasa (v. 1). They would be anxious to see how the keepers of swine (obviously Gentiles, since this was an occupation prohibited to Jews) might react to Jesus (vv. 11-17). They would recognize in this event Mark's way of describing the initial step in Christianity's spread to the Gentiles. Indeed, the Christian faith of Mark's day, which was adhered to by Jew and non-Jew alike, was rooted in Jesus' own loving outreach. Christianity had no limiting boundaries of race or nationality. Jesus' saving word and power were intended for all of God's people.

side, a large crowd gathered around him, and he stayed close to the sea. ²²One of the synagogue officials, named Jairus, came forward. Seeing him he fell at his feet ²³and pleaded earnestly with him, saying, "My daughter is at the point of death. Please, come lay your hands on her that she may get well and live." ²⁴He went off with him, and a large crowd followed him and pressed upon him.

²⁵There was a woman afflicted with hemorrhages for twelve years. ²⁶She had suffered greatly at the hands of many doctors and had spent all that she had. Yet she was not helped but only grew worse. ²⁷She had heard about Jesus and came up behind him in the crowd and touched his cloak. ²⁸She said, "If I but touch his clothes, I shall be cured." ²⁹Immediately her flow of blood dried up. She felt in her body that she was healed of her affliction. ³⁰Jesus, aware at once that power had gone out from him, turned around in the crowd and asked, "Who has touched my clothes?" ³¹But his disciples said to him, "You see how the crowd is pressing upon you, and yet you ask, 'Who touched me?'" ³²And he looked around to see who had done it. ³³The woman, realizing what had happened to her, approached in fear and trembling. She fell down before Jesus and told him the whole truth. ³⁴He said to her, "Daughter, your faith has saved you. Go in peace and be cured of your affliction."

³⁵While he was still speaking, people from the synagogue official's house arrived and said, "Your daughter has died, why trouble the teacher any longer?" ³⁶Disregarding the message that was re-

5:21-43 Jesus and women: life and trust. In Mark's Gospel Jesus is closely involved with women nine times. Here in verses 21-43, Mark's readers enter into two of Jesus' more moving encounters with women (Jairus' daughter and the woman with the hemorrhage). Both stories begin with someone seeking out Jesus, the healer. Both stories end in the cure of a person who had been hopelessly sick. Even the way Mark intertwines the two stories (the story of Jairus' daughter begins, the account of the hemorrhaging woman is related in full, and the Jairus story is then completed) shows that Mark wants his readers to hear one important message common to both: "Do not be afraid; just have faith" (v. 36)! The father of the little girl trusts Jesus even after hearing the report that she is dead (vv. 35-40). He is invited to witness Jesus' healing touch and word, and then sees his little girl walking around alive (vv. 41-42). The woman shows her trust by touching Jesus (v. 27) and by coming forward in spite of her fear (v. 33). She learns that her faith is rewarded by peace and lasting health (v. 34). Like Jairus and the woman, Christians of every age are urged by Mark to approach Jesus confidently with their earnest appeals on behalf of the sick and dying.

Even as he reports Jesus' miraculous power, Mark preserves the human side of Jesus. For example, the one who has more healing power than the physicians of his day (he cured the woman who had spent all her money and twelve years of time going to doctors, who failed to help her, v. 26) did not know who touched him (v. 30). Likewise, the one who raises the

ported, Jesus said to the synagogue official, "Do not be afraid; just have faith." [37]He did not allow anyone to accompany him inside except Peter, James, and John, the brother of James. [38]When they arrived at the house of the synagogue official, he caught sight of a commotion, people weeping and wailing loudly. [39]So he went in and said to them, "Why this commotion and weeping? The child is not dead but asleep." [40]And they ridiculed him. Then he put them all out. He took along the child's father and mother and those who were with him and entered the room where the child was. [41]He took the child by the hand and said to her, "*Talitha koum,*" which means, "Little girl, I say to you, arise!" [42]The girl, a child of twelve, arose immediately and walked around. [At that] they were utterly astounded. [43]He gave strict orders that no one should know this and said that she should be given something to eat.

6 The Rejection at Nazareth. [1]He departed from there and came to his native place, accompanied by his disciples.

little girl from her deathbed (v. 41) is also sensitive to her need for something to eat (v. 43). Such details make Mark's Jesus very approachable. He was not a perfect human (for example, he did not know everything), but he was perfectly human (he was full of compassion). Mark's readers can trust him now as those in need did when he walked on this earth. He is sensitive to the needs of those who seek him out.

It is important that Mark's readers notice the details in this passage that point to the climax of the Gospel. Such hints reveal Mark's desire to keep his readers moving with Jesus to the place where his journey leads. For example, Peter, James, and John, who witness the raising of the dead girl here, will soon question what "to rise from the dead" means (9:10). Likewise, the fearful, trembling woman with a hemorrhage points to the three women who will leave the empty tomb "seized with trembling and bewilderment," so afraid that they say nothing to anyone (16:8). There is almost no section of Mark's Gospel that does not draw his readers to its conclusion. Mark asks his readers, women and men, to stay with Jesus to the end. Even when life's confusion and tragedies get them down, Mark's readers are reminded: "Fear is useless. What is needed is trust in God, who brings life, even from death."

OF BREAD AND BLINDNESS

Mark 6:1–8:26

In chapters 1 to 5 Mark has highlighted Jesus' miracles and power over cosmic forces: over demons, over raging seas and winds, over sickness and death. He has also let his readers know that the proper Christian response to Jesus' power is faith in him, not terror or fear (4:40 and 5:36). In chapters 6 to 8 Mark will continue his picture of the powerful Jesus. However, he

²When the sabbath came he began to teach in the synagogue, and many who heard him were astonished. They said, "Where did this man get all this? What kind of wisdom has been given him? What mighty deeds are wrought by his hands! ³Is he not the carpenter, the son of Mary, and the brother of James and Joses and Judas and Simon? And are not his sisters here with us?" And they took offense at him. ⁴Jesus said to them, "A prophet is not without honor except in his native place and among his own kin and in his own house." ⁵So he was not able to perform any mighty deed there, apart from curing a few sick people by laying his hands on them. ⁶He was amazed at their lack of faith.

The Mission of the Twelve. He went around to the villages in the vicinity teaching. ⁷He summoned the Twelve and began to send them out two by two and

will emphasize even more how blind Jesus' disciples are to the meaning of Jesus' power (6:52 and 8:14-21).

Mark's readers will also notice a new emphasis in these chapters, namely, the breads. In chapters 6 to 8 Mark will repeatedly connect bread with the disciples' lack of understanding of Jesus. It gradually becomes clear that Mark is suggesting to his Christians that they will recognize the true meaning of Jesus for themselves only when they realize what their Eucharistic sharing of the bread really means. (The Eucharist commemorates their union with the risen Lord, who came to his glory through his suffering and death.) It is by "bread and blindness" that Mark's Jesus leads his followers to the half-way point and first climax of the Gospel, that is, to the revelation by Jesus to Peter and the disciples that the road to his final glory (and theirs) is by way of much suffering and death (8:27-38).

6:1-6 He was too much for them in Nazareth . . . and they for him! Jesus' disciples are with him as he teaches a large synagogue crowd in his hometown, Nazareth. While many of Mark's readers are interested in this passage because of its reference to Jesus' "brothers and sisters" (v. 3), Mark's own interest lay elsewhere. (Because of the Catholic church's teaching on the virginity of Mary, this mention of Jesus' brothers and sisters causes questions to be asked. However, neither this section nor 3:31-35, where his brothers and sisters are mentioned again, says anything definitive about Mary's virginity or Jesus' blood family, because in Mark's day "brothers and sisters" could refer to cousins, stepbrothers or stepsisters, or members of the extended family, as well as to blood sisters or brothers.) Mark passes on the account of the hometown folks' rejection of Jesus for a special reason: to provide an important transition and surprising contrasts at this point of his drama. The passage is transitional, for it bridges the greatest of Jesus' miracles (raising the girl from death) with the sharing of his healing power with the disciples (6:7-13). The surprising contrasts lie not so much in his town's

gave them authority over unclean spirits. ⁸He instructed them to take nothing for the journey but a walking stick—no food, no sack, no money in their belts. ⁹They were, however, to wear sandals but not a second tunic. ¹⁰He said to them, "Wherever you enter a house, stay there until you leave from there. ¹¹Whatever place does not welcome you or listen to you, leave there and shake the dust off your feet in testimony against them." ¹²So they went off and preached repentance. ¹³They drove out many demons, and they anointed with oil many who were sick and cured them.

Herod's Opinion of Jesus. ¹⁴King Herod heard about it, for his fame had become widespread, and people were saying, "John the Baptist has been raised from the dead; that is why mighty powers

rejection of him ("A prophet is not without honor . . .," v. 4) as in his discouragement and ineffectiveness in their midst: "So he was not able to perform any mighty deed there, apart from curing a few. . . . He was amazed at their lack of faith" (v. 5). Up to this point people have always been amazed and fearful in Jesus' presence. Here Jesus is amazed at them and at the lack of faith he finds in Nazareth. Mark's readers, no matter how familiar they are with Jesus, might well evaluate the depth of their faith in him in order to allow him to be as effective as he wants to be in their midst.

6:7-13 The apostles are sent to preach and to expel demons. Rejected by his own, Jesus preaches elsewhere and sends his twelve disciples out with special instructions and powers. The reader will remember that Mark has carefully prepared for this important moment when Jesus sends the apostles out. First, he had Jesus call them personally (1:16-20). Then he selected twelve special ones to accompany him (3:13-19). The Twelve, tutored by Jesus and present with him as he healed many from sickness and evil (chs. 3–5), are now ready to become "ones sent out" (the Greek word for "apostle" means "one sent out"). The specific order to expel unclean spirits (v. 7) is accompanied by further details regarding clothing, what to bring, where to stay, and what to do when they are rejected (vv. 8-11). These detailed directions were indications for the early church of the need to move quickly and to be dependent on God's care. Were Mark's Christians in A.D. 70 as trusting in God as Jesus called his Twelve to be? What are the specific apostolic mission orders for today's apostles who read Mark's Gospel? One thing seems clear: Mark is asking all his readers to consider prayerfully how to balance their eager action in building up God's kingdom with their trust in God's own loving involvement in their lives.

6:14-29 King Herod, John the Baptist, and Jesus. This rather long account of the death of John seemingly interrupts the flow of Mark's story about Jesus. However, it is likely that Mark presents this account here in order to prepare his readers for Jesus' death, much in the same way that John's

are at work in him." [15]Others were saying, "He is Elijah"; still others, "He is a prophet like any of the prophets." [16]But when Herod learned of it, he said, "It is John whom I beheaded. He has been raised up."

The Death of John the Baptist. [17]Herod was the one who had John arrested and bound in prison on account of Herodias, the wife of his brother Philip, whom he had married. [18]John had said to Herod, "It is not lawful for you to have your brother's wife." [19]Herodias harbored a grudge against him and wanted to kill him but was unable to do so. [20]Herod feared John, knowing him to be a righteous and holy man, and kept him in custody. When he heard him speak he was very much perplexed, yet he liked to listen to him. [21]She had an opportunity one day when Herod, on his birthday, gave a banquet for his courtiers, his military officers, and the leading men of Galilee. [22]Herodias's own daughter came in and performed a dance that delighted Herod and his guests. The king said to the girl, "Ask of me whatever you wish and I will grant it to you." [23]He even swore [many things] to her, "I will grant you whatever you ask of me, even to half of my kingdom." [24]She went out and said to her mother, "What shall I ask for?" She replied, "The head of John the Baptist." [25]The girl hurried back to the king's presence and made her request, "I want you to give me at once on a platter the head of John the Baptist." [26]The king was deeply distressed, but because of his oaths and the guests he did not wish to break his word to her. [27]So he promptly dispatched an executioner with orders to bring back his head. He went off and beheaded him in the prison. [28]He brought in the head on a platter and gave it to the girl. The girl in turn gave it to her mother. [29]When his disciples heard about it, they came and took his body and laid it in a tomb.

The Return of the Twelve. [30]The apostles gathered together with Jesus and first appearance in the Gospel prepared for Jesus' coming on the scene (1:2-11). A careful reading will indicate how John's death was truly a foretelling of Jesus' own death. Consider the clues. Although Herod was wrong about John being "raised up" (v. 16), Jesus will indeed be raised up (16:6-8). Like Herodias (v. 19), the chief priests want to kill Jesus but have to go about it by devious means because of what the people might do (11:18 and 14:1-2). Like Herod (v. 20), Pilate will have Jesus put to death even though he does not know what crime Jesus has committed (15:14). Finally, like John's disciples (v. 29), a follower of Jesus will get his dead body and "lay it in a tomb" (15:46). Such clues show that Mark wants his readers to see the fate of their Lord in the fate of his forerunner John. Mark also wants his readers to be so much like John, preparing others for the experience of Jesus in their lives and in death, that people will confuse them with Jesus too. Herod thought that Jesus was John come back to life. Will others think that Jesus has come back to life when they witness the life of Mark's Christian community, then and now?

6:30-52 Crowds, breads, and the walk on the water. The short passage in 6:30-33 serves to "round off" the missioning of the Twelve (in 6:7-13).

reported all they had done and taught. [31]He said to them, "Come away by yourselves to a deserted place and rest a while." People were coming and going in great numbers, and they had no opportunity even to eat. [32]So they went off in the boat by themselves to a deserted place. [33]People saw them leaving and many came to know about it. They hastened there on foot from all the towns and arrived at the place before them.

The Feeding of the Five Thousand. [34]When he disembarked and saw the vast crowd, his heart was moved with pity for them, for they were like sheep without a shepherd; and he began to teach them many things. [35]By now it was already late and his disciples approached him and said, "This is a deserted place and it is already very late. [36]Dismiss them so that they can go to the surrounding farms and villages and buy themselves something to eat." [37]He said to them in reply, "Give them some food yourselves." But they said to him, "Are we to buy two hundred days' wages worth of food and give it to them to eat?" [38]He asked them, "How many loaves do you have? Go and see." And when they had found out they said, "Five loaves and two fish." [39]So he gave orders to have them sit down in groups on the green grass. [40]The people took their places in rows by hundreds and by fifties. [41]Then, taking the five loaves and the two fish and looking up to heaven, he said the blessing, broke the loaves, and gave them

It also prepares Mark's readers for the rest of chapter 6, which features two closely related and marvelous manifestations of Jesus' identity as their Lord: first, as the one who feeds his people abundantly (with bread, 6:34-44); secondly, as the one who is with them in the most serious conflicts of their lives (on the raging sea, 6:45-52).

Although the apostles need time alone with Jesus (v. 31), he responds first to the greater need of the crowd that has found his place of refuge (v. 33). The first miracle of the breads (6:34-44) reveals for Mark and the early church that Jesus is as powerful and as loving as the God of Exodus 16, who provided manna for his wandering people in the desert. When Jesus pities them, "for they were like sheep without a shepherd" (v. 34), he becomes for Mark's readers the Good Shepherd of Ezekiel 34, tending his needy flock and teaching them at great length (v. 34). These allusions to the Old Testament remind Mark's readers of God's providence in the past. When, however, Mark has Jesus take the loaves, raise his eyes to heaven, pronounce a blessing, break the loaves, and give them to the disciples to distribute (v. 41), Mark's Christians become conscious of their present experience of the Lord in the Eucharist. The details of Jesus' *past* care for his hungry people are experienced in the *present* when his needy followers come to him for nourishment. Mark's readers share in the abundance of leftovers (v. 43)! God cares for God's people in Eucharist!

Immediately after the multiplication of the loaves, Mark presents a second scene in which Jesus calms a wind-swept sea on behalf of his fearful disciples (6:45-52; recall 4:35-41). As the wind begins to toss the boat around,

to [his] disciples to set before the people; he also divided the two fish among them all. [42]They all ate and were satisfied. [43]And they picked up twelve wicker baskets full of fragments and what was left of the fish. [44]Those who ate [of the loaves] were five thousand men.

The Walking on the Water. [45]Then he made his disciples get into the boat and precede him to the other side toward Bethsaida, while he dismissed the crowd. [46]And when he had taken leave of them, he went off to the mountain to pray. [47]When it was evening, the boat was far out on the sea and he was alone on shore. [48]Then he saw that they were tossed about while rowing, for the wind was against them. About the fourth watch of the night, he came towards them walking on the sea. He meant to pass by them. [49]But when they saw him walking on the sea, they thought it was a ghost and cried out. [50]They had all seen him and were terrified. But at once he spoke with them, "Take courage, it is I, do not be afraid!" [51]He got into the boat with them and the wind died down. They were [completely] astounded. [52]They had not understood the incident of the loaves. On the contrary, their hearts were hardened.

Jesus comes walking toward them on the water (v. 48; in 4:38 Jesus was in the boat with them, but he slept). Jesus' calming of the sea *and* the disciples (vv. 50-51) would be further signs for Mark and his readers that Jesus was their Lord of creation. Only God had such mastery over the sea (e.g., Gen 1:1-10). Only "I AM" had the power to divide the Red Sea for the Hebrew people (Exod 3:14 and 14:21). Even the strange phrase "He meant to pass by them" (v. 48) would point to Jesus' identity as Lord. (In Exod 33:22, God set Moses in the hollow of the rock and covered him with his hand until *he had passed by*. This was to protect Moses from seeing God's face, which meant death in Old Testament times.) Although Jesus intended to "pass by them," he reveals a new way of God's protecting the chosen people: he comes to be with those who are afraid. He assures them with his word: "IT IS I!"

The back-to-back miracles of the breads and the walk on the water would seem to be enough to convince anyone that God was once more among the people in the person of Jesus. However, when Mark says that the hearts of Jesus' disciples were hardened (v. 52), it seems that he is looking for something more from his readers. He hopes that they will question their own degree of intimacy with their risen Lord. In their own wind-tossed times, some forty years after Jesus' death and resurrection, would the reassuring words of Jesus ("Do not be afraid!") be enough for them? Or was the fear of the first disciples still present in the Christian community? Mark hopes that his readers will come to understand the meaning of *all* the events, including Jesus' humiliating death, as they understand more about the loaves. He hopes that their fears will be resolved when, at the Eucharist, they come to understand their own suffering in the light of Jesus' sacrifice for them and for all his people.

The Healings at Gennesaret. ⁵³After making the crossing, they came to land at Gennesaret and tied up there. ⁵⁴As they were leaving the boat, people immediately recognized him. ⁵⁵They scurried about the surrounding country and began to bring in the sick on mats to wherever they heard he was. ⁵⁶Whatever villages or towns or countryside he entered, they laid the sick in the marketplaces and begged him that they might touch only the tassel on his cloak; and as many as touched it were healed.

7 The Tradition of the Elders. ¹Now when the Pharisees with some scribes who had come from Jerusalem gathered around him, ²they observed that some of his disciples ate their meals with unclean, that is, unwashed, hands. ³(For the Pharisees and, in fact, all Jews, do not eat without carefully washing their hands, keeping the tradition of the elders. ⁴And on coming from the marketplace they do not eat without purifying themselves. And there are many other things that they have traditionally observed, the purification of cups and jugs and kettles [and beds].) ⁵So the Pharisees and scribes questioned him, "Why do your disciples not follow the tradition of the elders but instead eat a meal with unclean hands?" ⁶He responded, "Well did Isaiah prophesy about you hypocrites, as it is written:

'This people honors me with their lips,
  but their hearts are far from me;
⁷In vain do they worship me,
  teaching as doctrines human precepts.'

6:53-56 The touch that heals. Chapter 6 ends with the summary statement that "as many as touched the tassle on his cloak were healed" (v. 56). What a contrast! The crowds (of vv. 53-56) ran to Jesus wherever he put in an appearance. His disciples, however, the ones closest to him, "were completely astounded . . . their hearts were hardened" (vv. 51-52). The enthusiastic crowds also stand in sharp contrast to the antagonistic Pharisees who gather around and against Jesus in chapter 7. This brief passage helps Mark's readers, who wish to be intimate disciples of Jesus, to focus their faith on the only one whose touch can heal them of the brokenness and lack of meaning in their lives.

7:1-23 Conflict over eating bread and serving God. After Mark has shown how successful Jesus' mission of healing among the crowds has been (6:53-56), he reminds his readers of the heavy cloud that hangs over his entire Gospel drama. He now reports the detailed and sharp conflict between Jesus and the Pharisees over the issue of what and how to eat properly. It was conflicts like this one (and those already recorded in 2:1–3:6) that would bring to completion the Pharisees' plot, how they might "put him to death" (3:6).

What Jesus teaches in this passage is as important for Mark's readers today as it was in A.D. 70. Jesus, presented here by Mark as the clever Jewish rabbi, turns the Pharisees' challenge about the manner in which his disciples prepared to eat bread (it is unlike their traditional rites of purification, vv. 2-5) into a wide-sweeping exposure of their "lip service" interpretation of God's

[8]You disregard God's commandment but cling to human tradition." [9]He went on to say, "How well you have set aside the commandment of God in order to uphold your tradition! [10]For Moses said, 'Honor your father and your mother,' and 'Whoever curses father or mother shall die.' [11]Yet you say, 'If a person says to father or mother, "Any support you might have had from me is *qorban*"' (meaning, dedicated to God), [12]you allow him to do nothing more for his father or mother. [13]You nullify the word of God in favor of your tradition that you have handed on. And you do many such things." [14]He summoned the crowd again and said to them, "Hear me, all of you, and understand. [15]Nothing that enters one from outside can defile that person; but the things that come out from within are what defile."[[16]]

[17]When he got home away from the crowd his disciples questioned him about the parable. [18]He said to them, "Are even you likewise without understanding? Do you not realize that everything that goes

law (quoting Isa 29:13 in vv. 6-7). He continues with a second example of their false piety, the *qorban* tradition, which would deny parents the care due them by their children (vv. 9-13). (Scholars are hard pressed to find such a lack of filial piety in Jewish rabbinic tradition, which indicates that this *qorban* tradition was probably some extreme and isolated circumstance of Jesus' or Mark's day.)

Finally, Mark's Jesus expresses the timeless principle that it is not what or how one eats that makes a person clean or unclean. It is what comes from inside the depths of the person that makes one pure or impure (v. 15). Then, as if Jesus' stance were not clear enough, Mark has Jesus explain his powerful one-liner to his disciples. External things, like the food one eats, do not make a person evil. It is one's actions, inspired from within, that show when a person is not living according to God's commands (see the list in vv. 17-23). Mark hopes that his readers will look to the various ways they are living in relationship with others to see if they are responding to God "from within" (with their whole being) or merely with "lip service" (with superficial nods to tradition).

Why Mark presents this heavy conflict passage here is just as important as the message it contains. This conflict section interrupts a chain of six miracle stories (it comes after the feeding of the multitude, the walk on the water, and the healing of the crowds; it is followed by the healing of the Canaanite child, the cure of the deaf-mute, and the second feeding of the multitude). Mark seems to have at least two reasons for doing this. First, this heightens the tension of his drama, suggesting that anyone who chooses to follow Jesus as healer will be involved in many conflicts for the sake of the gospel, perhaps even with religious leaders and structures. Secondly, the conflict passage builds on his theme of the slow-witted disciples, because they need special tutoring again (here in v. 17), as they did earlier (in 4:10, 34). Thus Mark

43

into a person from outside cannot defile, [19]since it enters not the heart but the stomach and passes out into the latrine?" (Thus he declared all foods clean.) [20]"But what comes out of a person, that is what defiles. [21]From within people, from their hearts, come evil thoughts, unchastity, theft, murder, [22]adultery, greed, malice, deceit, licentiousness, envy, blasphemy, arrogance, folly. [23]All these evils come from within and they defile."

The Syrophoenician Woman's Faith. [24]From that place he went off to the district of Tyre. He entered a house and wanted no one to know about it, but he could not escape notice. [25]Soon a woman whose daughter had an unclean spirit heard about him. She came and fell at his feet. [26]The woman was a Greek, a Syrophoenician by birth, and she begged him to drive the demon out of her daughter. [27]He said to her, "Let the children be fed first. For it is not right to take the food of the children and throw it to the dogs." [28]She replied and said to him, "Lord, even the dogs under the table eat the children's

challenges Christian leaders within his audience to reevaluate the way they understand and pass on the Christian tradition entrusted to them.

7:24-37 Non-Jewish women and men are healed and spread the news. The two miracle stories that conclude chapter 7 are linked by the now familiar Markan theme of Jesus' desire for secrecy (see the comment on 1:32-34). Before healing the Syro-Phoenician's daughter, "he entered a house and wanted no one to know about it" (v. 24). After curing the deaf-mute, "he ordered them not to tell anyone" (v. 36). Of course, people *did* recognize him. They *did* spread the news of his healing power (vv. 24, 36-37). But even as Mark faithfully and readily records the marvels that Jesus performed, his secrecy theme does not allow his readers to forget that the true glory and identity of their Lord was only fully revealed in the death he underwent on their behalf.

The Syro-Phoenician woman who asked Jesus to heal her possessed daughter would seem to have had two counts against her from the start. Being a woman and a non-Jew, it is no wonder that she crouched at the feet of this male Jewish preacher, begging him for help (vv. 25-26)! The first-century readers of Mark's Gospel would not be overly surprised at Jesus' harsh-sounding refusal to give to Gentiles (the dogs) what rightfully belonged to the Jews (the children of the household). They would be surprised, though, that Jesus would allow a Gentile woman to persist in her pleading and even play off his own words to get what she wanted: "Lord, even the dogs under the table eat the children's scraps!" (vv. 27-28). Her persistence forces Jesus to make an exception to the rule (i.e., take care of your own people first, then go to others, v. 27). He cures her possessed daughter by a word as a reward for her mother's staying power and faith in him (v. 29).

Mark's readers would hear in this passage several invitations to action: first, to imitate the persistence of the woman, even when things seem hope-

scraps." [29]Then he said to her, "For saying this, you may go. The demon has gone out of your daughter." [30]When the woman went home, she found the child lying in bed and the demon gone.

The Healing of a Deaf Man. [31]Again he left the district of Tyre and went by way of Sidon to the Sea of Galilee, into the district of the Decapolis. [32]And people brought to him a deaf man who had a speech impediment and begged him to lay his hand on him. [33]He took him off by himself away from the crowd. He put his finger into the man's ears and, spitting, touched his tongue; [34]then he looked up to heaven and groaned, and said to him, *"Ephphatha!"* (that is, "Be opened!") [35]And [immediately] the man's ears were opened, his speech impediment was removed, and he spoke plainly. [36]He ordered them not to tell anyone. But the more he ordered them not to, the more they proclaimed it. [37]They were exceedingly astonished and they said, "He has

less; second, to imitate Jesus' "breaking the rules" on behalf of an "outsider"; and third, to examine their openness to those of other faiths, especially the Jews, the first "sons and daughters of the household."

The story of the deaf-mute is like a gate swinging back and forth. It swings back to the story of the Syro-Phoenician woman, because the deaf-mute also comes from a non-Jewish part of Palestine (v. 31). It swings forward to the next chapter, to the story of the blind man (8:22-26), which closely parallels this cure. Both the deaf-mute and the blind man are brought to Jesus by others (v. 32; 8:22). Both times Jesus takes the men away from the crowd (v. 33; 8:23) and touches them, using spittle to heal them (vv. 33-35 and 8:23, 25).

These obvious parallels make it clear that Mark wants the two cures to be read side by side. In this way, Mark's readers will hardly be able to miss that Jesus is the Messiah promised by Isaiah long before when he said: "Then will the eyes of the blind be opened, the ears of the deaf be cleared" (Isa 35:5-6; see Mark 7:37). However, with the final parallel element in the two stories (Jesus' request for secrecy in 7:37 and 8:26), Mark asks his readers to remember another Isaian passage that Jesus has fulfilled by his life and life-giving death: "Who would believe what we have heard? . . . He was spurned and avoided by all, a man of suffering, accustomed to infirmity . . . . pierced for our offenses, crushed for our sins. Upon him was the chastisement that makes us whole, by his stripes we were healed" (Isa 53:1-5).

Jesus, for Mark, was the perfect fulfillment of all Isaiah's prophecies. He was the promised Messiah who healed the deaf, the mute, and the blind. He was also the innocent one who suffered on behalf of his people. For Mark and his readers, Jesus is the one who says: "Follow me on my way. Care for my people, until there are no longer any sick or hurting people on this earth. But know that in your healing service of others you will experience the same pain that I experienced in making you whole. Stay with me. I will provide the nourishment you need" (see 8:1-10, which follows).

done all things well. He makes the deaf hear and [the] mute speak."

8 **The Feeding of the Four Thousand.** ¹In those days when there again was a great crowd without anything to eat, he summoned the disciples and said, ²"My heart is moved with pity for the crowd, because they have been with me now for three days and have nothing to eat. ³If I send them away hungry to their homes, they will collapse on the way, and some of them have come a great distance." ⁴His disciples answered him, "Where can any-

one get enough bread to satisfy them here in this deserted place?" ⁵Still he asked them, "How many loaves do you have?" "Seven," they replied. ⁶He ordered the crowd to sit down on the ground. Then, taking the seven loaves he gave thanks, broke them, and gave them to his disciples to distribute, and they distributed them to the crowd. ⁷They also had a few fish. He said the blessing over them and ordered them distributed also. ⁸They ate and were satisfied. They picked up the fragments left over—seven baskets.

8:1-10 Jesus feeds the crowd again. The second time that Mark's compassionate Jesus feeds the hungry crowds (8:1-9; recall 6:34-44) is another foreshadowing of the Eucharist (14:22-26), so important to Mark and to his community. Some readers think that this is the report of an actual second feeding incident (noting that there are many *differences* from the first feeding, e.g., the numbers of people and loaves, the different geographical locale, etc.). Others wonder if this might be a second written version of one and the same feeding event, pointing out the *similarities* in the two accounts, e.g., the pity Jesus feels, the similar words and gestures he uses, the same basic marvelous deed performed, etc. They also point to the disciples' question in 8:4 and believe that it makes no sense if the disciples have just seen Jesus feed five thousand people with five loaves in chapter 6.

Whatever the solution to this debate, it is fairly clear that Mark has included this second feeding account to make sure that the Gentile members of his community know they are welcomed to the Eucharist from the very beginning. (Notice that Jesus is still in Gentile territory at this point, 7:24, 31, and 8:10. Notice also the phrase in verse 3, "Some of them have come a great distance," i.e., "from afar," which is a well-known early Christian way of referring to Gentile converts.) Mark thus claims that Jesus is the giver of bread, ready to satisfy hungry followers of whatever background. He also suggests that the Christian Eucharist is the place for true Christian community to form, where people of diverse backgrounds become one in the Lord who gives bread to all in great abundance.

Was Mark's first audience in need of hearing that the Eucharist was meant to gather various segments of that community together? Are the readers of Mark's Gospel today in need of the same message, as people of the various Christian churches struggle to become one again in worship as well as in mission? Perhaps Mark wants all his readers to hear Jesus say: "Today my

⁹There were about four thousand people.

He dismissed them ¹⁰and got into the boat with his disciples and came to the region of Dalmanutha.

The Demand for a Sign. ¹¹The Pharisees came forward and began to argue with him, seeking from him a sign from heaven to test him. ¹²He sighed from the depth of his spirit and said, "Why does this generation seek a sign? Amen, I say to you, no sign will be given to this generation." ¹³Then he left them, got into the boat again, and went off to the other shore.

The Leaven of the Pharisees. ¹⁴They had forgotten to bring bread, and they had only one loaf with them in the boat. ¹⁵He enjoined them, "Watch out, guard against the leaven of the Pharisees and the leaven of Herod." ¹⁶They concluded among themselves that it was because they had no bread. ¹⁷When he became

heart is moved with pity *for you*. You hunger for unity. I want you to 'become one body, one spirit' in me" (Eucharistic Prayer III).

8:11-13 This age seeks a sign. This brief encounter with the Pharisees is little more than a transition passage. It links the second feeding (8:1-10) with the scene of Jesus in the boat with his disciples, asking them *eight* times to try to understand who he really is (8:14-21). Yet, this small transitional passage serves the purpose of heightening even more the severely strained relationship between Jesus and the Pharisees. It is wrought with emotion and tension. In Matthew's version (Matt 12:38-42), Jesus gives a clear, self-possessed answer to the Pharisees' demand for a sign: they shall be given the sign of "the prophet Jonah," signifying Jesus' three days in the tomb before his resurrection. Here in Mark's version, Jesus only "sighs from the depths of his spirit" (v. 12). He leaves them, without satisfying their desire for any words or actions concerning a "heavenly sign."

In this way, Mark portrays a Jesus who is so human, so much like his readers, that they could identify with him in his frustration with the religious leaders of his day, just as they have identified with him in his pity for the hungry crowd in the preceding passage. Mark's Jesus is one like them in all things. They will be like him in all things, even in frustrating conflicts with the unbelieving religious leaders of their day.

8:14-21 Jesus seeks recognition and understanding. In two previous episodes on the sea (4:35-41 and 6:45-52), Jesus has revealed himself as Lord over the sea, and in both cases his disciples' "hearts were hardened" (6:52). Once again on the lake with them, Jesus wants them to see who he is. This time he instructs them to keep their eyes open and not to be like the bad "leaven of the Pharisees and the leaven of Herod" (v. 15). (The latter saw Jesus as a popular wonder-worker who threatened their authority as religious and political leaders of the people.) Since the disciples "had forgotten to bring bread along," they missed Jesus' point about the leaven of the Pharisees (vv. 14 and 16). Consequently, with a barrage of eight questions,

aware of this he said to them, "Why do you conclude that it is because you have no bread? Do you not yet understand or comprehend? Are your hearts hardened? [18]Do you have eyes and not see, ears and not hear? And do you not remember, [19]when I broke the five loaves for the five thousand, how many wicker baskets full of fragments you picked up?" They answered him, "Twelve." [20]"When I broke the seven loaves for the four thousand, how many full baskets of fragments did you pick up?" They answered [him], "Seven." [21]He said to them, "Do you still not understand?"

The Blind Man of Bethsaida. [22]When they arrived at Bethsaida, they brought to him a blind man and begged him to touch him. [23]He took the blind man by the hand and led him outside the village. Putting spittle on his eyes he laid his hands on him and asked, "Do you see anything?" [24]Looking up he replied, "I see people looking like trees and walking." [25]Then he laid hands on his eyes a second time and he saw clearly; his sight was restored and he could see everything distinctly. [26]Then he sent him home and said, "Do not even go into the village."

Jesus makes his followers realize that they misunderstand him as much as the Pharisees do (v. 17). They who were with him as he healed the deaf-mute (7:31-37) have ears but are not hearing (v. 18). They who were witnesses of his feeding the multitudes with bread (chs. 6 and 8) "still do not understand" that he alone is enough nourishment for them (v. 21).

When Jesus asks how much bread is left over (v. 20), it marks the seventeenth time that the breads have been mentioned in chapters 6 to 8 and the last time bread occurs until the Last Supper scene at 14:22. As the end of the "Bread and Blindness" section of his Gospel draws near, Mark hopes that his readers will examine their appreciation of the Christian community's celebration of the Eucharist. He also invites them to see, to hear, and to understand the many ways that their Lord (the "one loaf" of v. 14?) wants to be involved in their lives.

8:22-26 A blind man sees perfectly, gradually. By now, the fact that Jesus heals yet another person is nothing special to the readers of Mark's Gospel. However, to anyone following the developing threads of the Gospel drama to this point, this is a very special cure. That is because this is the first blind person to be healed. He is also healed "in stages," just before the passage in which Peter and the disciples begin to get a glimpse of the way Jesus must go (vv. 27-38). These special details lead Mark's readers to the realization that the blind man of chapter 8 is much more than an individual whom Jesus cured in A.D. 30. He is the symbol of the first disciples and of all disciples of Jesus, ever in need of his enlightening touch. Mark's readers have begun to see more clearly. Are they ready to go forward with Jesus on his way?

III: THE MYSTERY BEGINS TO BE REVEALED

Peter's Confession about Jesus. [27]Now Jesus and his disciples set out for the villages of Caesarea Philippi. Along the way he asked his disciples, "Who do people say that I am?" [28]They said in reply, "John the Baptist, others Elijah, still others one of the prophets." [29]And he asked them, "But who do you say that I am?" Peter

THE WAY OF JESUS BECOMES CLEARER

Mark 8:27–10:52

In the first eight chapters of his Gospel, Mark has portrayed the people around Jesus, both friend and foe, as people blind to the true meaning of his miraculous works (nineteen miraculous events conclude with 8:21: "Do you still not understand?"). What follows are two and a half tightly knit chapters, bound together by the blind-man story just concluded (8:22-26) and a second blind-man story that will end with the cured man following Jesus "on the way" to Jerusalem, the goal of his journey and the end of his way (10:52 and 11:1). Between these two "book-end" blind-man passages, Mark has placed three clear predictions of Jesus' passion, each followed by his disciples' continued lack of comprehension.

As these chapters unfold, so unfolds Jesus' revelation of himself as the one who will rise from the dead (in each of the predictions and in 9:2-9). But of course the disciples do not understand this either (9:10)! Perhaps the most important thing to happen in these chapters is the way in which Mark turns the various miracle stories and dialogues into opportunities for explicit "teaching moments" about the meaning of the Christian life and its radical demands. Thus, the miracles in the first half of the Gospel are replaced by hard teachings in the second half.

If there is any general call that the readers of these chapters will hear, it will be the call to be as trusting as little children in the service of others. (The word-fields of "little child" and "servant" dominate these chapters as "the breads" and "blindness" dominated chapters 6–8). Perhaps by the account of the second blind man's cure (end of ch. 10), those who *hear* Jesus' message and teachings will finally *see* that the person they follow and the mission they share is radical but simple, tiring but transforming, impossible for them alone but not for God. His is a way of service and self-giving that gives life to others and preserves one's own.

8:27–9:1 Revelation of the way of the Messiah and his followers. As Mark's readers approach Caesarea Philippi with Jesus and his disciples (v. 27), they arrive at the first major climax of Mark's Gospel drama. (The second climax is the passion account, chs. 15–16). Until now, Mark has been

said to him in reply, "You are the Messiah." ³⁰Then he warned them not to tell anyone about him.

The First Prediction of the Passion. ³¹He began to teach them that the Son of Man must suffer greatly and be rejected by the elders, the chief priests, and the scribes, and be killed, and rise after three days. ³²He spoke this openly. Then Peter took him aside and began to rebuke him. ³³At this he turned around and, looking at his disciples, rebuked Peter and said, "Get behind me, Satan. You are thinking not as God does, but as human beings do."

The Conditions of Discipleship. ³⁴He summoned the crowd with his disciples and said to them, "Whoever wishes to

revealing who Jesus is in the mighty deeds he has done. Along with this revelation, Mark has also reported Jesus' reluctance to have people believe in him only because of those wondrous deeds. (Recall the "secret" of 8:26; 7:36; 5:43, etc.) This Caesarea Philippi passage is the heart of the matter. Jesus now says explicitly that his way is a way of suffering. The way of the Messiah is the way of the cross.

Mark, Matthew, and Luke all record this important passage. However, whereas Peter's confession of faith gets rewarded with "the keys to the kingdom of heaven" in Matthew's Gospel (Matt 16:19), Mark only reports that Peter is told not to tell anyone that Jesus is the Messiah (v. 30). Mark knew what Peter meant by "Messiah," namely, "the powerful deliverer of God." Mark also knew that Jesus understood that title differently, i.e., that it signified that he was "the Son of Man, [who] must suffer greatly and be rejected . . . be killed, and rise after three days" (v. 31).

The account goes on to show that Peter and the disciples were not ready for this. They wanted a leader who would deliver them from pain, not one who would experience pain and death himself! Consequently, Peter rebukes Jesus (v. 32), angering Jesus to the point of sending Peter away as if he were the devil himself (v. 33). Indeed, when Mark shifts the focus of the scene from Peter to the crowd and the disciples (v. 34), his readers find out that they also must share the disciples' struggle with the hard, cold reality that Jesus is not the "instant cure-all" person they would like him to be. They can hear him speak directly to them, saying: "Whoever wishes to come after me, must deny himself or herself, take up the cross, and follow in my steps!" (v. 34).

Even today's reader finds it hard to swallow the absolute and radical statements that follow: "For whoever wishes to save her/his life will lose it . . . ." (v. 35); "What could one give in exchange for one's life!" (v. 37). Yes, says Mark, *all* who call themselves followers of Jesus must lose their lives for Jesus' sake and the sake of the gospel (v. 35). Mark thus pushes his readers to the edge. Either they give themselves in total trust to the suffering Messiah they

come after me must deny himself, take up his cross, and follow me. ³⁵For whoever wishes to save his life will lose it, but whoever loses his life for my sake and that of the gospel will save it. ³⁶What profit is there for one to gain the whole world and forfeit his life? ³⁷What could one give in exchange for his life? ³⁸Whoever is ashamed of me and of my words in this faithless and sinful generation, the Son of Man will be ashamed of when he comes in his Father's glory with the holy angels."

9 ¹He also said to them, "Amen, I say to you, there are some standing here who will not taste death until they see that the kingdom of God has come in power."

The Transfiguration of Jesus. ²After six days Jesus took Peter, James, and John and led them up a high mountain apart by themselves. And he was transfigured before them, ³and his clothes became dazzling white, such as no fuller on earth could bleach them. ⁴Then Elijah appeared to them along with Moses, and they were conversing with Jesus. ⁵Then Peter said

follow, or they open themselves up to the awful prospect of hearing an unfavorable judgment: "The Son of Man will be ashamed of them when he comes in his Father's glory with the holy angels" (v. 38).

Although Mark's readers in A.D. 70 were not among those standing there in A.D. 30 (9:1), his urgent challenge was still theirs, because "the kingdom of God coming in power" could be upon them at any time. Likewise, although twentieth-century readers of Mark's Gospel might not share his expectations of an imminent return of Jesus in glory and judgment, the urgency of this whole section of his Gospel does provoke profound questions for individual Christians and for the whole church. If Mark's readers are to take his Jesus seriously, how can they begin today to live the Christian life more radically? What are the times and circumstances in which they can be people of gospel values in the midst of their world today? Mark's Jesus will respond to these questions with some concrete means in chapters 9 and 10. For now, Mark allows his readers to sit back and respond to these questions before he takes them up a high mountain with Peter, James, and John (9:2-8).

9:2-13 Revelation of glory (and suffering). It almost seems that Mark knows his readers will be exhausted after the encounter at Caesarea Philippi, because he follows it six days later with one of the most refreshing and consoling events of his Gospel—the transfiguration. Jesus takes Peter, James, and John up the mountain with him, the same three whom he had brought with him when he restored the little girl to life (v. 2; recall 5:37-40). The three have a glimpse of Jesus in his dazzling glory (v. 3). When they see him conversing with Elijah and Moses, they are awe-struck at the realization that Jesus is the fulfillment of the prophets (Elijah) and of all the law (Moses).

Peter wants to capture the consoling moment and keep Jesus, Moses, and Elijah there with them (v. 5). However, Mark does not allow his readers to linger on the mountaintop any longer than Peter, James, and John do. In-

to Jesus in reply, "Rabbi, it is good that we are here! Let us make three tents: one for you, one for Moses, and one for Elijah." [6]He hardly knew what to say, they were so terrified. [7]Then a cloud came, casting a shadow over them; then from the cloud came a voice, "This is my beloved Son. Listen to him." [8]Suddenly, looking around, they no longer saw anyone but Jesus alone with them.

The Coming of Elijah. [9]As they were coming down from the mountain, he charged them not to relate what they had seen to anyone, except when the Son of Man had risen from the dead. [10]So they kept the matter to themselves, questioning what rising from the dead meant. [11]Then they asked him, "Why do the scribes say that Elijah must come first?" [12]He told them, "Elijah will indeed come first and restore all things, yet how is it written regarding the Son of Man that he must suffer greatly and be treated with contempt? [13]But I tell you that Elijah has come and they did to him whatever they pleased, as it is written of him."

The Healing of a Boy with a Demon. [14]When they came to the disciples, they saw a large crowd around them and scribes arguing with them. [15]Immediately

stead, God's voice from the cloud repeats what it had said earlier at Jesus' baptism: "This is my beloved Son" (1:11). Then the voice adds: "Listen to him!" (v. 7). Mark's readers do not have to think hard to remember what Jesus has spoken for them to hear (8:34–9:1). Their refreshing pause on the mountain is over. Glimpses and tastes of glory that Christians receive from God are real, but according to Mark, they are given so that Christians can move on with him, and with him alone (v. 8).

Any enlightenment that Peter, James, and John received on the mountain seems dulled as Mark reports the conversation they have with Jesus on the way down (vv. 9-13). Jesus knew, says Mark, that they would have difficulty accepting the fact that he would have to suffer and die before rising from the dead. Consequently, he tells them not to get themselves or others excited about the glory of the transfiguration event until after he has risen from the dead (v. 9). They ask about the role Elijah is to play in the restoration of God's people, to which Jesus responds with a question of his own about the suffering role of the Son of Man (v. 12). Then he answers their question, saying that Elijah has already come and fulfilled his role (1 Kgs 19:2-10; likewise, Mark's Jesus is referring to John the Baptist as "Elijah, his forerunner"). Thus, as this section ends, Peter, James, and John, as well as Mark's readers, are left to respond to Jesus' unanswered question (v. 12): "Why does Scripture say of the Son of Man that he must suffer greatly and be treated with contempt?"

9:14-29 "I do believe! Help my unbelief!" The healing of the possessed boy is one of the longest miracle stories in Mark's Gospel (only the expulsion of the demons in 5:1-20 is longer). It is also one of the more detailed stories, becoming a bit complicated in the repetition of some of those details

on seeing him, the whole crowd was utterly amazed. They ran up to him and greeted him. ¹⁶He asked them, "What are you arguing about with them?" ¹⁷Someone from the crowd answered him, "Teacher, I have brought to you my son possessed by a mute spirit. ¹⁸Wherever it seizes him, it throws him down; he foams at the mouth, grinds his teeth, and becomes rigid. I asked your disciples to drive it out, but they were unable to do so." ¹⁹He said to them in reply, "O faithless generation, how long will I be with you? How long will I endure you? Bring him to me." ²⁰They brought the boy to him. And when he saw him, the spirit immediately threw the boy into convulsions. As he fell to the ground, he began to roll around and foam at the mouth. ²¹Then he questioned his father, "How long has this been happening to him?" He replied, "Since childhood. ²²It has often thrown him into fire and into water to kill him. But if you can do anything, have compassion on us and help us." ²³Jesus said to him, " 'If you can!' Everything is possible to one who has faith." ²⁴Then the boy's father cried out, "I do believe, help my unbelief!" ²⁵Jesus, on seeing a crowd rapidly gathering, rebuked the unclean spirit and said to it, "Mute and deaf spirit, I command you: come out of him and never enter him again!" ²⁶Shouting and throwing the boy into convulsions, it came out. He became like a corpse, which caused many to say, "He is dead!" ²⁷But Jesus took him by the hand, raised him, and he stood up. ²⁸When he entered the house, his disciples asked him in private, "Why could we not drive it out?" ²⁹He said to them, "This kind can only come out through prayer."

The Second Prediction of the Passion.
³⁰They left from there and began a jour-

(e.g., in v. 22 the father of the boy tells Jesus what he has *already* told him in v. 18; the crowd gathers twice within the same story in vv. 15 and 25). Despite its length and detail, there is a very clear and simple message that Mark wishes to convey: Anything is possible to one who trusts (v. 23), and trust is deepened by prayer (v. 29)!

Although Jesus is the one who heals the boy (vv. 25-27), it is the father's profession of faith that Mark holds up for his readers to imitate. Even in the most desperate moments, when prayer and trust seem useless, Jesus invites his followers to go one step further and pray like the boy's father: "I do believe! Help my unbelief!" (v. 24). Perhaps the alert reader of the Gospel will hear the echoes of Jesus' message all along (e.g., "Do not be afraid; just have faith" in 5:36; "Please, Lord, even the dogs under the table eat the children's scraps" in 7:28), calling for a persistent and ever more radical trust in him. The same theme will carry over into the following passages, in which the total trust of little children becomes the model of what is needed to take part in the kingdom of God (9:35-37 and 10:13-16).

9:30-32 The second (of three) predictions of death and resurrection. Jesus' disciples were not able to expel the demon from the young boy (9:18) because of the lack of belief among the people (9:19) and because of their own lack of prayerfulness (9:29). Is it surprising, then, that the disciples will fail to understand the meaning of Jesus' second prediction of his death and

ney through Galilee, but he did not wish anyone to know about it. [31]He was teaching his disciples and telling them, "The Son of Man is to be handed over to men and they will kill him, and three days after his death he will rise." [32]But they did not understand the saying, and they were afraid to question him.

IV: THE FULL REVELATION OF THE MYSTERY

The Greatest in the Kingdom. [33]They came to Capernaum and, once inside the house, he began to ask them, "What were you arguing about on the way?" [34]But they remained silent. They had been discussing among themselves on the way who was the greatest. [35]Then he sat down, called the Twelve, and said to them, "If anyone wishes to be first, he shall be the last of all and the servant of all."[36]Taking a child he placed it in their midst, and putting his arms around it he said to them, [37]"Whoever receives one child such as this in my name, receives me; and whoever receives me, receives not me but the one who sent me."

Another Exorcist. [38]John said to him, "Teacher, we saw someone driving out demons in your name, and we tried to prevent him because he does not follow us." [39]Jesus replied, "Do not prevent him.

resurrection (vv. 31-32)? Mark's note that "they were afraid to question him" about this prediction (v. 32) might help his readers to deal with the fact that the Twelve abandoned Jesus in his passion and death. It might also encourage his readers to pause, take stock of their own fears, and confidently express them in prayer with their Lord.

9:33-50 Some radical demands of discipleship. Each evangelist records those teachings of Jesus that meet the needs of his readers. Here we notice some concerns that Mark hopes his community will face: (1) ambition among themselves (vv. 33-37); (2) envy and intolerance of others (vv. 38-41); and (3) scandalizing others (vv. 42-48).

The first concern, the evil of ambition, is a major one for Mark as pastor of his community. (This becomes even clearer in chapter 10 when the third passion prediction is followed by another warning against ambition, 10:35-45). How ambitious Jesus' disciples are! They argue about who is the most important among them (9:33-34) instead of trying to understand the meaning of their leader's passion prediction (9:32)! The response of Jesus (and Mark) is direct and simple: to be "important" among Jesus' followers means to be a humble servant, not a proud "first" (v. 35). In verses 36-37 Mark's Jesus presents himself and the child as models of openness to others: "Whoever receives one child such as this in my name receives me." What a contrast this is to the disciples' interests (in v. 34)! How different from their closed attitudes toward others (in vv. 38-42)!

Mark's second concern, the pettiness of arrogance and envy, is exposed when John and other disciples try to exclude a "non-member" from doing ministry in the name of Jesus (v. 38). Jesus (and Mark) challenge the dis-

There is no one who performs a mighty deed in my name who can at the same time speak ill of me. ⁴⁰For whoever is not against us is for us. ⁴¹Anyone who gives you a cup of water to drink because you belong to Christ, amen, I say to you, will surely not lose his reward.

Temptations to Sin. ⁴²"Whoever causes one of these little ones who believe [in me] to sin, it would be better for him if a great millstone were put around his neck and he were thrown into the sea. ⁴³If your hand causes you to sin, cut it off. It is better for you to enter into life maimed than with two hands to go into Gehenna, into the unquenchable fire.[⁴⁴] ⁴⁵And if your foot causes you to sin, cut it off. It is better for you to enter into life crippled than with two feet to be thrown into Gehenna. [⁴⁶] ⁴⁷And if your eye causes you to sin, pluck it out. Better for you to enter into the kingdom of God with one eye than with two eyes to be thrown into Gehenna, ⁴⁸where 'their worm does not die, and the fire is not quenched.' "

The Simile of Salt. ⁴⁹"Everyone will be salted with fire. ⁵⁰Salt is good, but if salt becomes insipid, with what will you restore its flavor? Keep salt in yourselves and you will have peace with one another."

10 **Marriage and Divorce.** ¹He set out from there and went into the district of Judea [and] across the Jordan. Again crowds gathered around him and, as was his custom, he again taught them.

ciples to be tolerant and open to others of good will: Working in Jesus' name brings its reward to anyone who "is not against us!" (vv. 40-41).

A third concern, the danger of causing scandal to others (v. 42), is met by Jesus' (and Mark's) harsh, traditional imagery of the unquenchable fires of Gehenna (vv. 43-48). In order to avoid those fires, Jesus' followers must be extremely cautious of giving bad example to anyone. Indeed, it would be better to cut off an arm or leg and enter heaven maimed than to give scandal to others and be thrown into hell!

Mark concludes this demanding section of his Gospel with a confusing but powerful mixed metaphor. Jesus claims that his followers will be cleansed ("salted" by the fire of v. 49) so that they can be at peace within and with others (the useful, tasty salt of v. 50). He thus presents a highly seasoned mixture of challenges to his own disciples and readers in A.D. 70 and today. His readers must reflect upon the liveliness of their gospel spirit. They must also root out the evils of ambition, envy, and scandal wherever they exist in their midst.

10:1-12 The Pharisees ask about divorce; Jesus responds. Journeying south from Capernaum (see 9:33), Jesus finally comes to Judea (10:1), on his way up to Jerusalem (10:32). In Judea, Jesus continues to preach his demanding message (begun in 8:34-38 and 9:33-50). However, in chapter 10 there seems to be an intentional attempt on Mark's part to establish a certain pattern and rhythm that gradually build up to the climax of his Gospel. The Markan arrangement consists of three passages in which Jesus meets with individual characters (the Pharisees of v. 2; the young man of v. 17; and

²The Pharisees approached and asked, "Is it lawful for a husband to divorce his wife?" They were testing him. ³He said to them in reply, "What did Moses command you?" ⁴They replied, "Moses permitted him to write a bill of divorce and dismiss her." ⁵But Jesus told them, "Because of the hardness of your hearts he wrote you this commandment. ⁶But from the beginning of creation, 'God made them male and female. ⁷For this reason a man shall leave his father and mother [and be joined to his wife], ⁸and the two shall become one flesh.' So they are no longer two but one flesh. ⁹Therefore what God has joined together, no human being must separate." ¹⁰In the house the disciples again questioned him about this. ¹¹He said to them, "Whoever divorces his wife and marries another commits adul-

James and John in v. 35). Then Mark's Jesus uses the encounters to teach his Twelve privately (v. 10, v. 23, and v. 41). These three similar passages are rhythmically balanced by three interspersed "models" for the Christian disciple to imitate (the child of vv. 13-16; Jesus himself in vv. 32-34; and the blind man in vv. 46-52).

The first encounter of chapter 10 has to do with the ever important issue of the fidelity of spouses in the marriage relationship (vv. 1-12). The early church was careful to preserve Jesus' attitudes concerning significant matters of daily living. Here Mark passes on the earliest tradition of Jesus' attitude toward marriage and divorce (vv. 6-9). While other teachers allowed men to divorce their wives in certain circumstances, Jesus taught that it was not permissible "to separate what God has joined together," using Gen 1:27 and 2:24 as authority for his interpretation. In other words, the Jesus tradition made it clear that it was not permissible for a man to divorce his wife. After Jesus talks privately with the Twelve (v. 10), Mark passes on what had come to be the earliest adaptation of Jesus' words for the Christian community, namely, if a man or a woman should have to divorce his or her spouse, he or she could not remarry without being considered an adulterer (vv. 11-12).

In these few verses, today's readers of Mark's Gospel can see the early church's struggle with one of the most painful areas of concern in the contemporary church and society—the meaning of fidelity in marriage relationships. At the core of Mark's Gospel message is Jesus' challenge to spouses to live in faithful and perpetual union until death. At the same time, recognizing the hard reality of life, even this early Gospel seems to allow for the separation (without remarriage, however) of spouses who can no longer love one another as husband or wife. (Matthew's Gospel, at 19:9, adds another "exception clause," which shows how this vital issue was dealt with in Matthew's community.) Thus, there are some whom Mark's Jesus will challenge to continue to be faithful forever. There are others whom he will challenge

tery against her; [12]and if she divorces her husband and marries another, she commits adultery."

Blessing of the Children. [13]And people were bringing children to him that he might touch them, but the disciples rebuked them. [14]When Jesus saw this he became indignant and said to them, "Let the children come to me; do not prevent them; for the kingdom of God belongs to such as these. [15]Amen, I say to you, whoever does not accept the kingdom of God like a child will not enter it." [16]Then he embraced them and blessed them, placing his hands on them.

The Rich Man. [17]As he was setting out on a journey, a man ran up, knelt down before him, and asked him, "Good teacher, what must I do to inherit eternal life?" [18]Jesus answered him, "Why do you call me good? No one is good but God alone. [19]You know the commandments: 'You shall not kill; you shall not commit adultery; you shall not steal; you shall not bear false witness; you shall not defraud; honor your father and your

to adapt, as the early church did, to the needs and feelings of those who no longer can live with their spouses.

10:13-16 The model of the child: total trust. Perhaps Jesus' teaching concerning fidelity in marriage inspired Mark to follow that passage (10:1-12) with the image of the child (vv. 13-16). Mark claims in these verses that only a childlike trust will enable his Christians to live up to Jesus' demands in the concrete day-to-day relationships they have, in the family and elsewhere. Once more the disciples seem to want to avoid hearing the truth. They scold the people for bringing children to Jesus (v. 13). In turn, Jesus' human compassion is aroused to passionate indignation with them. Only Mark records Jesus' anger with the disciples and his tender touching of the children (vv. 14 and 16; compare Matt 19:14-15).

When Jesus says that it is only to those who are as needy and receptive as children that the kingdom of God belongs (vv. 14-15), he invites his readers to delve more deeply into the realization of their own human helplessness. Only thus can the power of their God and Father live in them. The positive acceptance of one's own powerlessness and God's power draws Mark's readers very close to the experience of having the kingdom of God established in their hearts. As Jesus will say in the next section of the Gospel, "For human beings it is impossible but not for God. All things are possible for God" (10:27).

10:17-31 The rich man asks about everlasting life; Jesus looks at him with love. In Matthew's version of this encounter, Jesus tells the rich man: "If you wish to be perfect, go, sell what you have, and give to the poor" (Matt 19:21). In Mark's account there is no "if" clause. The one who wants to follow Mark's Jesus must give up all he or she has, give the proceeds to the poor, and then follow him (v. 21). What a demanding person Mark's Jesus is! Here is an eager, prospective disciple, who has kept all the com-

mother.' " ²⁰He replied and said to him, "Teacher, all of these I have observed from my youth." ²¹Jesus, looking at him, loved him and said to him, "You are lacking in one thing. Go, sell what you have, and give to [the] poor and you will have treasure in heaven; then come, follow me." ²²At that statement his face fell, and he went away sad, for he had many possessions.

²³Jesus looked around and said to his disciples, "How hard it is for those who have wealth to enter the kingdom of God!" ²⁴The disciples were amazed at his words. So Jesus again said to them in reply, "Children, how hard it is to enter the kingdom of God! ²⁵It is easier for a camel to pass through [the] eye of [a] needle than for one who is rich to enter the kingdom of God." ²⁶They were exceedingly astonished and said among themselves, "Then who can be saved?" ²⁷Jesus looked at them and said, "For human beings it is impossible, but not for God. All things are possible for God." ²⁸Peter began to say to him, "We have given up everything and followed you." ²⁹Jesus said, "Amen, I say to you, there is no one who has given up house or brothers or sisters or mother or father or children or land for my sake and for the sake of the gospel ³⁰who will not receive a hundred times more now in this present age: houses and brothers and sisters and mothers and children and lands, with persecutions, and eternal life in the age to come. ³¹But many

mandments since his childhood (v. 20). He wants everlasting life (v. 17). Jesus looks on him with love, but then challenges him beyond his capacities (see v. 22: "He went away sad, for he had many possessions").

Mark's Jesus turns to his disciples and makes it clear to them that having many possessions is an almost insurmountable deterrent to possession of the kingdom of God (vv. 23-25). This overwhelmed Jesus' disciples (v. 26) and probably overwhelmed Mark's first readers as thoroughly as it challenges his readers today. Mark calls for the trust of the child in its parents: "All things are possible for God" (v. 27; recall the model of the child in 10:13-16). However, that challenging response did not satisfy Peter, just as it probably did not satisfy Mark's Christians, who had already left so much to follow Jesus (v. 28). In verses 29-31, Mark assures his readers that anyone who is detached from everything and everyone, so that he or she can follow after Jesus, will receive a hundredfold of family members and possessions in this life, while inheriting everlasting life in the age to come. (Mark's readers will note that those who leave all for Jesus will also receive "persecutions," v. 30. Even when he assures his Christians of their reward, Mark's Jesus reminds them that they stand in the shadow of the cross.)

In the world of today, just as in the time of Jesus and Mark, security in possessions and in money can pull people away from depending on God as the true source of their life, here and hereafter. Like the man in the Gospel story, all of Mark's Christians are called to radical discipleship. To follow Jesus still means to go and sell what one has. To be for Jesus still means to be for the poor. The man in the Gospel story wanted everlasting life. The

that are first will be last, and [the] last will be first."

The Third Prediction of the Passion. [32]They were on the way, going up to Jerusalem, and Jesus went ahead of them. They were amazed, and those who followed were afraid. Taking the Twelve aside again, he began to tell them what was going to happen to him. [33]"Behold, we are going up to Jerusalem, and the Son of Man will be handed over to the chief priests and the scribes, and they will condemn him to death and hand him over to the Gentiles [34]who will mock him, spit upon him, scourge him, and put him to death, but after three days he will rise."

Ambition of James and John. [35]Then James and John, the sons of Zebedee, came to him and said to him, "Teacher, we want you to do for us whatever we ask of you." [36]He replied, "What do you wish [me] to do for you?" [37]They an-

Christian way to everlasting life is to be poor. Jesus' way is to rely solely on God, for whom all things are possible!

10:32-34 The "Suffering Servant" predicts his fate for the third time. Mark records Jesus' third and final prediction of his death and resurrection, with some details that were missing in the previous two predictions: it would happen in Jerusalem; and the Gentiles would mock him, spit at him, and flog him before killing him (vv. 33-34). As the end of Jesus' way draws closer, the more explicitly he identifies himself with the suffering servant of Isaiah, who would heal his people by the very stripes, chastisement, and harsh treatment he would endure for their sakes (Isa 53:1-7).

The manner in which Mark sets the scene for this third prediction is significant: "They were on the way, going up to Jerusalem, and Jesus went ahead of them" (v. 32). Jesus knows where they are headed and what awaits him in Jerusalem. But the disciples follow, "amazed," and the crowd trails along in fear. By this time the reader must wonder what effect such predictions had on the first disciples, especially when two of the Twelve (James and John) show that they have completely misunderstood what he has said (see next passage, 10:35-45). Mark hopes that his unfolding Gospel drama will have a more lasting effect on his Christian readers. He hopes that they will consciously choose to model their lives on Jesus, the Suffering Servant, who walks ahead of them.

10:35-45 James and John ask about glory; Jesus gives them the cross. The request of James and John to sit at Jesus' right and left in glory makes up the next to last scene before Jesus arrives in Jerusalem, the place of his death. It seems almost impossible that these two disciples could ask such an ambitious and inappropriate question after Mark's Jesus has been describing his way of suffering so clearly, since 8:31! (Matthew casts James and John in a better light, having their mother pose the request, Matt 20:20.)

Jesus responds to their request with a challenging question of his own: "Can you drink the cup I shall drink or be baptized with the baptism with

swered him, "Grant that in your glory we may sit one at your right and the other at your left." ³⁸Jesus said to them, "You do not know what you are asking. Can you drink the cup that I drink or be baptized with the baptism with which I am baptized?" ³⁹They said to him, "We can." Jesus said to them, "The cup that I drink, you will drink, and with the baptism with which I am baptized, you will be baptized; ⁴⁰but to sit at my right or at my left is not mine to give but is for those for whom it has been prepared." ⁴¹When the ten heard this, they became indignant at James and John. ⁴²Jesus summoned them and said to them, "You know that those who are recognized as rulers over the Gentiles lord it over them, and their great ones make their authority over them felt. ⁴³But it shall not be so among you. Rather, whoever wishes to be great among you will be your servant; ⁴⁴whoever wishes to be first among you will be the slave of all. ⁴⁵For the Son of

which I am baptized?" (v. 38). Since "the cup" and "baptism" language is symbolic for Mark of Jesus' agony and death to come, it is obvious that Jesus is challenging James and John to take very seriously what it means to follow him to glory. Then, in response to their eager "We can" of v. 39, Jesus divides the issue: You shall share in my cup, in my baptism, in my death. But it is up to someone else, my Father, to give out the seats of glory! (v. 40).

Jesus thus concludes the dialogue in such a way that James and John get a profound (and unwanted?) answer to their ambitious request. The answer is not a simple "yes" or "no," but a challenge: "Perhaps the Father will reserve the seats for you, *if* you willingly take on my cross, my cup, my baptism." Who among Mark's readers in A.D. 70 or today is eager to go "all the way" with Jesus?

Verse 41 is the transition verse by which Mark draws his own Christian readers more explicitly into the dialogue. Today's reader of the incident might become indignant with James and John, as the other ten disciples did, and say, "How selfish they are!" However, Mark's Jesus calls *all* of his followers together and says: "It is not only in this one incident that Christians manifest selfish, unchristian attitudes. Whoever wants to follow the Son of Man must take an uncompromising stance against such non-gospel values as 'lording it over others'" (v. 42). To be a Christian is to be a servant, as Jesus was (v. 45). To be first and greatest is to serve the needs of all, as Jesus did (v. 44). That is the way to glory for a disciple of Mark's Jesus!

Because this scene features James and John, two of Jesus' most intimate disciples (remember that they were with him at the transfiguration, 9:2-9, and that they will be with him in the garden of his agony, 14:32-42), Mark's message here is especially relevant to anyone in a leadership position in the church. It is a "servant leadership" that Mark calls for. The church's leaders are meant to be the first to "drink the cup," daily serving the needs of their brothers and sisters, whatever those needs are, whenever they are perceived.

Man did not come to be served but to serve and to give his life as a ransom for many."

The Blind Bartimaeus. ⁴⁶They came to Jericho. And as he was leaving Jericho with his disciples and a sizable crowd, Bartimaeus, a blind man, the son of Timaeus, sat by the roadside begging. ⁴⁷On hearing that it was Jesus of Nazareth, he began to cry out and say, "Jesus, son of David, have pity on me." ⁴⁸And many rebuked him, telling him to be silent. But he kept calling out all the more, "Son of David, have pity on me." ⁴⁹Jesus stopped and said, "Call him." So they called the blind man, saying to him, "Take courage; get up, he is calling you." ⁵⁰He threw aside his cloak, sprang up, and came to Jesus. ⁵¹Jesus said to him in reply, "What do you want me to do for you?" The blind man replied to him, "Master, I want to see." ⁵²Jesus told him,

If this call seems too radical and even impossible to fulfill, Mark next offers his readers the example of someone else—the blind beggar Bartimaeus of verses 46-52—who probably thought his situation was hopeless.

10:46-52 The model of the blind man: "I want to see!" The cure of blind Bartimaeus concludes this demanding section of Mark's Gospel drama, just as the cure of the other blind man (8:22-26) concluded the "Bread and Blindness" chapters (6–8). In contrast to the first blind man, who was brought to Jesus by others (8:22), Bartimaeus cries out on his own initiative: "Jesus, Son of David, have pity on me!" (v. 47). The title he gives Jesus, "Son of David," indicates that he, a *blind* beggar, actually *sees who Jesus is* more clearly than the disciples and crowd who have been with him all along! Although some people try to quiet the man (v. 48), his persistence wins out. Jesus has his disciples call him closer (v. 49). Bartimaeus responds with great enthusiasm and comes to Jesus. He becomes the one and only person in Mark's Gospel who calls Jesus "Master." (This particular way of addressing Jesus appears in the New Testament only here and at John 20:16, when Mary Magdalene meets the risen Jesus near the empty tomb.)

In the Gospel of Matthew, the parallel story has two blind men call for Jesus' help; and Jesus, moved with compassion, *touched their eyes* (Matt 20:33-34). Here in Mark's version of the incident, Jesus need not touch Bartimaeus. He does not even have to say "Your faith has saved you" (as Luke has it, in 18:42), because Bartimaeus' cry and actions reveal his deep faith. Jesus is his master! It is just such profound trust in Jesus that Mark wants to elicit from the Christian recipients of his Gospel.

When the blind man immediately received his sight and started to follow Jesus "on the way" (v. 52), Mark offers a smooth transition to the next section of the Gospel (i.e., the *end* of the road, Jerusalem and Calvary, chs. 11–15). More important, however, he offers his community the hope and encouraging example of this early disciple of Jesus (the phrase "to follow him on the way" was a familiar designation for discipleship in the early church).

"Go your way; your faith has saved you."
Immediately he received his sight and followed him on the way.

11 **The Entry into Jerusalem.** ¹When
they drew near to Jerusalem, to
Bethphage and Bethany at the Mount of

Olives, he sent two of his disciples ²and
said to them, "Go into the village opposite you, and immediately on entering it,
you will find a colt tethered on which no
one has ever sat. Untie it and bring it here.
³If anyone should say to you, 'Why are

Consequently, after Mark presents the very difficult teachings of Jesus about
the Christian attitude toward divorce, riches, and ambition (earlier in ch.
10), this miracle-discipleship story becomes Mark's rallying call to his Christian readers in their own situation, on their own way of the cross: "You have
nothing to fear from him! Get up! He is calling you!"

ON TO JERUSALEM

Mark 11:1-13:37

This major section of Mark's Gospel begins with Jesus' entry into Jerusalem (11:1-11) and ends with his long discourse about the Jerusalem temple
and the "days of tribulation" (13:1-37). Throughout these three chapters,
Mark's readers will find themselves involved with Jesus in a series of fore-
boding incidents that build up to his betrayal, passion, and death in Jerusalem (chs. 14–15). Almost all of the scenes in chapters 11 to 13 are
conflict-ridden, showing Jesus in confrontation with the religious leaders of
Jerusalem over the issues of prayer and piety (11:12-25 and 12:28-44); life
after death (12:18-27); tribute due to Caesar (12:13-17); and Jesus' authority
in all such matters (11:27-33). This series of conflict stories will remind Mark's
readers of earlier conflicts (2:1–3:6), which ended with the Pharisees' plotting with the Herodians how they might destroy Jesus (3:6). This time the
plotting leads to his arrest and death (14:43-52 and 15:21-26).

By his choice of the various scenes for these three critical chapters, Mark
leaves no doubt in his readers' minds about what the basis of their Christian
discipleship is: they are to put their trust in God (11:22), and they must put
that trust into action by loving their neighbor as themselves (12:31). Their
models will be two: (1) the sincere scribe of 12:28-34 and (2) the poor widow,
whose generous trust in God urged her to give "from her poverty, all she
had, her whole livelihood" (12:44).

11:1-11 Jesus' entry into Jerusalem. Mark's account of Jesus' triumphal
entry into Jerusalem functions much as the transfiguration event did earlier
(9:2-8). It is another exhilarating moment on the otherwise long and ardu-
ous "way" of Jesus to his saving passion and death. Because Jerusalem was

The Mount of Temptation near Jericho, where Jesus was tempted by Satan (Mark 1:12-13)

Excavations at Jericho, twenty-four miles northeast of Jerusalem

The southeast corner of the wall of the Old City as seen on the Jericho road

"Go into the village opposite you, and immediately on entering it, you will find a colt tethered on which no one has ever sat" (Mark 11:2).

you doing this?' reply, 'The Master has need of it and will send it back here at once.' " ⁴So they went off and found a colt tethered at a gate outside on the street, and they untied it. ⁵Some of the bystanders said to them, "What are you doing, untying the colt?" ⁶They answered them just as Jesus had told them to, and they permitted them to do it. ⁷So they brought the colt to Jesus and put their cloaks over it. And he sat on it. ⁸Many people spread their cloaks on the road, and others spread leafy branches that they had cut from the fields. ⁹Those preceding him as well as those following kept crying out: "Hosanna!

Blessed is he who comes in the name of the Lord!
¹⁰Blessed is the kingdom of our father David that is to come!
Hosanna in the highest!"
¹¹He entered Jerusalem and went into the temple area. He looked around at everything and, since it was already late, went out to Bethany with the Twelve.

Jesus Curses a Fig Tree. ¹²The next day as they were leaving Bethany he was hungry. ¹³Seeing from a distance a fig tree in leaf, he went over to see if he could find anything on it. When he reached it he found nothing but leaves; it was not the time for figs. ¹⁴And he said to it in reply,

the holy city of God, and because the details of Jesus' arrival there (vv. 7-10) point to the coming of Israel's Prophet-Savior (e.g., "See, your king shall come . . . riding on an ass, on a colt, the foal of an ass," Zech 9:9), Mark's first readers would not be able to miss the obvious connection: *Jesus was the longed-for Savior of Israel!* They could join the crowds and shout: "Hosanna! The reign of God and of our father David has begun with Jesus' coming!"

However, because Jerusalem was also the city of Jesus' death, Mark is quick to play down the enthusiasm surrounding Jesus' entry. (This nuance in Mark's Gospel becomes evident when his account is compared with Matthew's version, which has "the very large crowd spread their cloaks on the road," Matt 21:8, and "the whole city was shaken" at his entry, Matt 21:10.) Consequently, the way Mark presents this episode allows his readers to rejoice in the risen Lord's kingship over them while not allowing them to forget the cost of being his disciples, namely, that they must deny their very selves, take up their cross, and follow in his steps (8:34).

The exhilarating moment of the entry into Jerusalem has come and gone. After a night's rest at Bethany with the Twelve, Jesus returns to the city for the final days and the final act of the Gospel drama (11:11-12).

11:12-25 The cursed fig tree and the cleansing of the temple. At first reading, the story of Jesus and the fig tree (vv. 12-14 and 20-21) is one of the strangest in the Gospels. It is uncharacteristic enough of Jesus to curse a fig tree for not having fruit on it. But when Mark includes the detail that "it was not the time for figs" (v. 13), Jesus appears even more unreasonable, and the incident becomes more difficult to understand.

"May no one ever eat of your fruit again!" And his disciples heard it.

Cleansing of the Temple. [15]They came to Jerusalem, and on entering the temple area he began to drive out those selling and buying there. He overturned the tables of the money changers and the seats of those who were selling doves. [16]He did not permit anyone to carry anything through the temple area. [17]Then he taught them saying, "Is it not written:

'My house shall be called a house of prayer for all peoples'?

But you have made it a den of thieves."

[18]The chief priests and the scribes came to hear of it and were seeking a way to put him to death, yet they feared him because the whole crowd was astonished at his teaching. [19]When evening came, they went out of the city.

The Withered Fig Tree. [20]Early in the morning, as they were walking along, they saw the fig tree withered to its roots. [21]Peter remembered and said to him, "Rabbi, look! The fig tree that you cursed has withered." [22]Jesus said to them in reply, "Have faith in God. [23]Amen, I say to you, whoever says to this mountain, 'Be lifted up and thrown into the sea,' and

Two keys are needed to unlock the meaning of this strange passage. First, Mark's readers may recall that the fig tree was a common Old Testament image for Israel (e.g., Hos 9:10). Therefore, Jesus' cursing of the tree would symbolically stand for his anger with the Jewish people. But why does Mark's Jesus curse Israel at this point of the Gospel drama? (Remember that the people have just welcomed him triumphantly into Jerusalem!) A second key to understanding this passage is its immediate context, which reveals an angry Jesus driving the buyers and sellers from the sacred temple area. They have turned what was meant to be "a house of prayer for all peoples" into a "den of thieves" (v. 17, quoting Isa 56:7). Consequently, Mark's readers can see why he wove the fig-tree passage together with the cleansing of the temple. The withered fig tree (v. 21) is meant to symbolize the fruitless side of Jewish temple piety in Jesus' time.

This passage might well challenge Mark's Christian readers to evaluate the depth of their own faith. In contrast to the superficial ceremony of the old temple, Mark hopes that they will have the type of profound trust in God that can move mountains (vv. 22-23). In verses 23-24, Mark's Jesus uses very bold, even exaggerated, language to say that by faith and prayer his people will be able to do what seems impossible, as well as receive *whatever* they ask for in prayer. (Remember the similarly strong "image with a point" in 10:25: "It is easier for a camel to pass through the eye of a needle than for one who is rich to enter the kingdom of God.")

Jesus and the early church believed in the infinite power of prayer. It seems that the only thing Mark's readers cannot hope to receive in prayer is an escape from their share in the suffering way of the Lord. For example: "Amen, I say to you, there is no one who has given up house or brothers or sisters or mother or father or children or lands for my sake and for the

does not doubt in his heart but believes that what he says will happen, it shall be done for him. ²⁴Therefore I tell you, all that you ask for in prayer, believe that you will receive it and it shall be yours. ²⁵When you stand to pray, forgive anyone against whom you have a grievance, so that your heavenly Father may in turn forgive you your transgressions.[²⁶]"

The Authority of Jesus Questioned. ²⁷They returned once more to Jerusalem. As he was walking in the temple area, the chief priests, the scribes, and the elders approached him ²⁸and said to him, "By what authority are you doing these things? Or who gave you this authority to do them?" ²⁹Jesus said to them, "I shall ask you one question. Answer me, and I will tell you by what authority I do these things. ³⁰Was John's baptism of heavenly or of human origin? Answer me." ³¹They discussed this among themselves and said, "If we say, 'Of heavenly origin,' he will say, '[Then] why did you not believe him?' ³²But shall we say, 'Of human origin'?"—they feared the crowd, for they all thought John really was a prophet. ³²So they said to Jesus in reply, "We do

sake of the gospel who will not receive a hundred times more now in this present age: houses and brothers and sisters and mothers and children and lands, *with persecutions,* and eternal life in the age to come (10:29ff.).

Mark concludes his description of Jesus' type of true piety by saying that anyone who prays with forgiveness for those who have offended them shall be forgiven in turn by the Father in heaven (v. 25). Although Mark does not relate the Our Father in his Gospel, as Matthew and Luke do, this little section brings out the attitudes of radical trust and forgiveness that are expected of God's children in their lives and in their prayer.

11:27-33 The lines of authority are drawn: conflict! The chief priests and scribes, who were looking for a way to destroy Jesus after he had cleansed the temple (11:18), question him "by what authority" he teaches and acts as he does (v. 28). This is not a simple question put by one teacher to another. It is a most serious challenge, the first in the final series of challenges that Jesus will face from the religious leaders of his day (11:27–12:44).

Mark's readers will notice how each conflict ends with a victorious Jesus silencing his opponents, the experts in Jewish law and scriptures. Here, for example, in verses 29-33, Jesus takes their question about his authority and turns it into his own clever question about the authority of John the Baptist (v. 30). Since the scribes feared what others, friends or foes of John, might think of their response (vv. 31-32), they are forced to admit: "We do not know" (v. 33). What began as a threat to Jesus' authority ends as an example of how little authority (and courage) his antagonists had! Mark wants his readers to take pride in the confounding wisdom of their teacher, Jesus. He also might be cleverly questioning his readers as to how they use the authority they possess in the church or how courageously they challenge the way others use the authority vested in them.

not know." Then Jesus said to them, "Neither shall I tell you by what authority I do these things."

12 **Parable of the Tenants.** ¹He began to speak to them in parables. "A man planted a vineyard, put a hedge around it, dug a wine press, and built a tower. Then he leased it to tenant farmers and left on a journey. ²At the proper time he sent a servant to the tenants to obtain from them some of the produce of the vineyard. ³But they seized him, beat him, and sent him away empty-handed. ⁴Again he sent them another servant. And that one they beat over the head and treated shamefully. ⁵He sent yet another whom they killed. So, too, many others; some they beat, others they killed. ⁶He had one other to send, a beloved son. He sent him to them last of all, thinking, 'They will respect my son.' ⁷But those tenants said to one another, 'This is the heir. Come, let us kill him, and the inheritance will be ours.' ⁸So they seized him and killed him, and threw him out of the vineyard. ⁹What [then] will the owner of the vineyard do? He will come, put the tenants to death, and give the vineyard to others. ¹⁰Have you not read this scripture passage:

'The stone that the builders rejected
has become the cornerstone;
¹¹by the Lord has this been done,
and it is wonderful in our eyes'?"
¹²They were seeking to arrest him, but they feared the crowd, for they realized that he had addressed the parable to them. So they left him and went away.

12:1-12 The parable of the vineyard: the rejected stone (son) is the cornerstone. For the first time since chapter 4, Mark has Jesus "speak to them in parables" (v. 1), namely, in the parable of the vineyard and the evil tenants (vv. 3-8). This is the last parable Mark records, and what a perfect last parable it is! By it, Mark anticipates the final act of his whole Gospel drama, since the rejection of the owner's son (v. 8) looks to the crucifixion of Jesus, and the reaction of the owner (vv. 9-11) points to the resurrection, when the Father vindicates Jesus' death.

Mark's Christian readers would understand the various elements and the deeper message of this parable as clearly as the scribes and chief priests to whom it was addressed ("They realized that he had addressed the parable to them," v. 12). The care of the vineyard (the people of Israel) had been entrusted by God to the leaders of the Jewish people (the "tenant farmers"). They treated the son (Jesus) as ruthlessly (vv. 6-8) as they had treated the Old Testament prophets before him (vv. 2-5). Because they did so, they no longer have any authority with God's new people. Rather, that authority now rests with the leaders of the early church (v. 9).

Mark conveys the same message when he has Jesus quote Psalm 118. Only the key image changes, namely, the "son" becomes the cornerstone (vv. 10-11). As Mark prepares his readers for their encounter with Jesus' death, he makes it clear where the blame for the Son's death lay—with the Jewish leaders. He also challenges Christian leaders to examine the relationship they have with Christ, "the cornerstone." For them, this parable is food for seri-

Paying Taxes to the Emperor. [13]They sent some Pharisees and Herodians to him to ensnare him in his speech. [14]They came and said to him, "Teacher, we know that you are a truthful man and that you are not concerned with anyone's opinion. You do not regard a person's status but teach the way of God in accordance with the truth. Is it lawful to pay the census tax to Caesar or not? Should we pay or should we not pay?" [15]Knowing their hypocrisy he said to them, "Why are you testing me? Bring me a denarius to look at." [16]They brought one to him and he said to them, "Whose image and inscription is this?" They replied to him, "Caesar's." [17]So Jesus said to them, "Repay to Caesar what belongs to Caesar and to God what belongs to God." They were utterly amazed at him.

The Question about the Resurrection. [18]Some Sadducees, who say there is no resurrection, came to him and put this question to him, [19]saying, "Teacher, Moses wrote for us, 'If someone's brother dies, leaving a wife but no child, his brother must take the wife and raise up descendants for his brother.' [20]Now there were seven brothers. The first married a woman and died, leaving no descendants. [21]So the second married her and died, leaving no descendants, and the third likewise. [22]And the seven left no descendants. Last of all the woman also died. [23]At the resurrection [when they arise] whose wife will she be? For all seven had been married to her." [24]Jesus said to them, "Are you not misled because you do not know the scriptures or the power of God? [25]When they rise from the dead, they nei-

ous thought about how they are caring for the church entrusted into their hands by the risen Lord.

12:13-27 Of tribute due to Caesar and to the living God. Mark moves from his last parable to two more of Jesus' conflict encounters with Jewish leadership. The first concerns the tax due to the emperor (vv. 13-17), and the second has to do with belief in resurrection and life after death (vv. 18-27). Mark's readers will discern a similar pattern in both encounters. First, the leaders approach Jesus with trick questions, obviously trying to "ensnare him in his speech" (v. 13). The Pharisees and Herodians ask if a good Jew should pay taxes to the Roman emperor or if that is against the law of Moses (v. 14). Then the Sadducees, who were known for not believing in the resurrection, ask a legalistic and cynical question about marriage relationships in the risen life (v. 23).

In response to their questions, Jesus shows a cunning wisdom that unveils their intent to trip him up. He exposes their hypocrisy in one case (v. 15) and shows their shallow understanding of their own Scriptures in the other (v. 24). Good Jews (and good Christians in Mark's audience) are expected to pay "tax tribute" to lawful civil leaders and "praise and true allegiance tribute" to God (vv. 15-17). Jews (and Christians) who really understand their sacred Scriptures should also know that "the God of Abraham, the God of Isaac, the God of Jacob" (and of the risen Jesus) is "not God of the dead but of the living" (vv. 24-27).

ther marry nor are given in marriage, but they are like the angels in heaven. ²⁶As for the dead being raised, have you not read in the Book of Moses, in the passage about the bush, how God told him, 'I am the God of Abraham, [the] God of Isaac, and [the] God of Jacob'? ²⁷He is not God of the dead but of the living. You are greatly misled."

The Greatest Commandment. ²⁸One of the scribes, when he came forward and heard them disputing and saw how well he had answered them, asked him, "Which is the first of all the command-

ments?" ²⁹Jesus replied, "The first is this: 'Hear, O Israel! The Lord our God is Lord alone! ³⁰You shall love the Lord your God with all your heart, with all your soul, with all your mind, and with all your strength.' ³¹The second is this: 'You shall love your neighbor as yourself.' There is no other commandment greater than these." ³²The scribe said to him, "Well said, teacher. You are right in saying, 'He is One and there is no other than he.' ³³And 'to love him with all your heart, with all your understanding, with all your strength, and to love your neighbor as

The cumulative result of these two encounters is that Mark's readers, like those first involved with Jesus, might be "amazed" at Jesus' wisdom (v. 17) and at his dedication to his Father, the God of life. But Mark wants more than amazement—he wants his Christians to imitate their Lord by being courageous apostles of truth and life themselves. How they are to be such apostles is up to them in their own circumstances. However, the following passage will give them a concrete model to follow.

12:28-34 The scribe who was close to the reign of God. After all the scheming and malicious questioning from the elders and scribes, for Jesus to claim that a scribe is "not far from the kingdom of God" (v. 34) is quite remarkable. Yet, upon examining this dialogue over which is the "first of all the commandments" (v. 28), Mark's readers can readily approve of the scribe's sincerity and honest attempt to understand the underlying basis of Jesus' way. Jesus responds to his question with the traditional *Shema* prayer, which every Israelite prays twice daily: "Hear, O Israel! The Lord our God is Lord alone!" (v. 29). Since the Lord is one, Jesus and the *Shema* continue, one's whole being (heart, soul, mind, and strength) should love God (v. 30). Jesus then adds a second command: "You shall love your neighbor as yourself." In effect, he makes the first of all the commandments into one dual commandment ("There is no greater commandment than *these*," v. 31).

The scribe appreciates Jesus' response. He sees how Jesus has combined two commands given to Israel by Moses (Deut 6:2 and Lev 19:18). He also hears in Jesus' response more than Jesus has said! He hears in it the echo of the prophet who declared that love, not sacrifice, is what God desires of all people (v. 33, quoting Hos 6:6).

Mark's readers know how correct the scribe was, because they knew that Jesus practiced what he taught. He had loved God and his neighbor unto

yourself' is worth more than all burnt offerings and sacrifices." ³⁴And when Jesus saw that [he] answered with understanding, he said to him, "You are not far from the kingdom of God." And no one dared to ask him any more questions.

The Question about David's Son. ³⁵As Jesus was teaching in the temple area he said, "How do the scribes claim that the Messiah is the son of David? ³⁶David himself, inspired by the holy Spirit, said:

'The Lord said to my lord,
"Sit at my right hand
    until I place your enemies under your
        feet." '

³⁷David himself calls him 'lord'; so how is he his son?" [The] great crowd heard this with delight.

Denunciation of the Scribes. ³⁸In the course of his teaching he said, "Beware of the scribes, who like to go around in long robes and accept greetings in the marketplaces, ³⁹seats of honor in synagogues, and places of honor at banquets. ⁴⁰They devour the houses of widows and, as a pretext, recite lengthy prayers. They will receive a very severe condemnation."

The Poor Widow's Contribution. ⁴¹He sat down opposite the treasury and observed how the crowd put money into the

death. His sacrifice was love! As they leave the crowds, who no longer "dared to ask him any more questions" (v. 34), Mark's readers might well ask themselves how their love of God is verified by their love of neighbor. They might ask how their sacrifice and liturgical worship of God are made manifest in their sacrifices for others. Mark's report of this encounter thus challenges his Christians to be like Jesus and also like this singular scribe, who had such insight into the ways of the kingdom. It also prepares them for the last two episodes of chapter 12, which will contrast the generous piety of the widow with the empty prayer of certain scribes (12:38-44).

12:35-37 Jesus is David's Lord and God's Son. Up to this point in chapter 12, the scribes have been asking Jesus challenging questions. He now asks them one: "How do [you] claim that the Messiah is the son of David" (v. 35), when David himself (in Ps 110:1) refers to the Messiah as "my Lord" (v. 36)? Mark's readers know that Jesus is their Messiah. They also know that he was of Davidic descent. However, Mark wants his readers to acknowledge even more, namely, that Jesus is the Son of God. Some people put Jesus to death because he claimed to be "the Son of the Blessed One" (14:61-64). How will Mark's readers renew their commitment to their Lord, who is also David's Lord and God's Son?

12:38-44 The poor widow shows the scribes the meaning of religion. The last time Mark presents Jesus in the temple is one of the most dramatic moments of his whole Gospel. Jesus first warns people to beware of the scribes, who pray long and loud in order to be seen and respected as "the holy ones" (vv. 38-39). At the same time, because they "devour the houses of widows" (v. 40), they show how empty their prayer is. (They also disobey a special commandment given to their ancestors by Moses: "You shall not wrong any widow or orphan or stranger," Exod 22:21.)

treasury. Many rich people put in large sums. ⁴²A poor widow also came and put in two small coins worth a few cents. ⁴³Calling his disciples to himself, he said to them, "Amen, I say to you, this poor widow put in more than all the other contributors to the treasury. ⁴⁴For they have all contributed from their surplus wealth, but she, from her poverty, has contributed all she had, her whole livelihood."

13 **The Destruction of the Temple Foretold.** ¹As he was making his way out of the temple area one of his disciples said to him, "Look, teacher, what stones and what buildings!" ²Jesus said to him, "Do you see these great buildings? There will not be one stone left upon another that will not be thrown down."

The Signs of the End. ³As he was sitting on the Mount of Olives opposite the

To this story of hypocrisy Mark has added the touching picture-example of the poor widow (vv. 41-44). Look at her, says Mark's Jesus. She puts much less money in the box than the wealthy ones (v. 41), "but she, from her poverty, has contributed all she had, her whole livelihood" (v. 44). Her offering is a sign of what total dependence on God really means. The widow thus becomes a model of faith for Mark's readers. If they imitate her generous and trusting faith, they will also be imitating Jesus, who likewise gave up his very life for the many (chs. 14-15)!

13:1-4 The end of the temple and the end of "all these things." As Jesus and the disciples leave the temple area, Mark has Jesus predict that "there will not be one stone [of these great buildings] left upon another" (v. 2). They respond to Jesus' remarkable statement with an important related question: "Tell us, when will this happen? And what sign will there be when all these things [i.e., the world as we know it] are about to come to an end?" Mark's readers today might not see how the disciples' question about the end of the world follows logically from Jesus' prediction about the end of the temple. They will understand the connection, however, if two significant facts are made clear: (1) the early church saw the destruction of Jerusalem as a pre-eminent sign of the soon-to-come end of the world; and (2) the early Christians for whom Mark was writing had *already* witnessed that destruction of Jerusalem (in A.D. 70 by the Roman army). Such historical background will help today's readers of Mark's Gospel understand this important chapter.

It is also helpful for Mark's readers to realize the special type of literature they will be involved with for the rest of chapter 13. All of Jesus' talk about "the end" and the signs that will accompany it belongs to the type of first-century writing known as "apocalyptic." In the early church, apocalyptic writing was used to communicate hope to fearful people by revealing how God would definitively save his faithful ones from any and all evil forces at the end of time. Apocalyptic literature made up a small (in content) but very significant (in meaning) part of Christianity's first gospel mes-

temple area, Peter, James, John, and Andrew asked him privately, 4"Tell us, when will this happen, and what sign will there be when all these things are about to come to an end?" 5Jesus began to say to them, "See that no one deceives you. 6Many will come in my name saying, 'I am he,' and they will deceive many. 7When you hear of wars and reports of wars do not be alarmed; such things must happen, but it will not yet be the end. 8Nation will rise against nation and kingdom against kingdom. There will be earthquakes from place to place and there will be famines. These are the beginnings of the labor pains.

The Coming Persecution. 9"Watch out for yourselves. They will hand you over to the courts. You will be beaten in synagogues. You will be arraigned before governors and kings because of me, as a witness before them. 10But the gospel must first be preached to all nations. 11When they lead you away and hand you over, do not worry beforehand about what you are to say. But say whatever

sage. (Such writing was rather common in certain Old Testament communities, which were longing for the coming of their Messiah to deliver them from foreign, pagan rulers. See, for example, the Book of Daniel, chapters 7–12, written about 150 B.C., which describes the coming of the Son of Man in terms very similar to those found here in Mark's Gospel. See also New Testament writings like Matt 24–25, Luke 21, 1 Thess 4–5, and the Book of Revelation, which reflect the early church's keen consciousness of the Lord's absence and its expectations of his imminent return in glory.) It is in chapter 13 that Mark passes on to his community the early church's hopeful preoccupation with Jesus' return. It is here that Mark describes the attitudes to be adopted by his readers in the time between Jesus' resurrection and that return.

13:5-23 Christian alertness and endurance in "the end times." Mark begins Jesus' apocalyptic speech with a section (vv. 5-23) that exemplifies very well two ways in which apocalyptic language is meant to move its readers to response and action. First, the catch phrase that begins and ends this section ("See that no one deceives you" at v. 5, and "Be watchful" at v. 23) signals his readers to be very alert to their response to certain misleading preachers in their midst ("who come in my name," v. 6, and "false messiahs and prophets," v. 22) who say the end is already here because of certain signs (for example, wars, v. 7; earthquakes, v. 8; persecution, vv. 9-13). The proper Christian response, says Mark, is not to panic (v. 7) but to persevere. Mark encourages his readers to view their perseverance in times of tension as a positive sign of God's protecting Holy Spirit with them until the end (vv. 9 and 11). Even more important, Mark demands that his readers be alert to means of spreading the good news about Jesus "to all nations" (v. 10), because only when that missionary effort is concluded can the end really come.

will be given to you at that hour. For it will not be you who are speaking but the holy Spirit. ¹²Brother will hand over brother to death, and the father his child; children will rise up against parents and have them put to death. ¹³You will be hated by all because of my name. But the one who perseveres to the end will be saved.

The Great Tribulation. ¹⁴"When you see the desolating abomination standing where he should not (let the reader understand), then those in Judea must flee to the mountains, ¹⁵[and] a person on a housetop must not go down or enter to get anything out of his house, ¹⁶and a person in a field must not return to get his cloak. ¹⁷Woe to pregnant women and nursing mothers in those days. ¹⁸Pray that this does not happen in winter. ¹⁹For those times will have tribulation such as has not been since the beginning of God's creation until now, nor ever will be. ²⁰If the Lord had not shortened those days, no one would be saved; but for the sake of the elect whom he chose, he did shorten the days. ²¹If anyone says to you then, 'Look, here is the Messiah! Look, there he is!' do not believe it. ²²False messiahs and false prophets will arise and will perform signs and wonders in order to mislead, if that were possible, the elect. ²³Be watchful! I have told it all to you beforehand.

The Coming of the Son of Man. ²⁴"But in those days after that tribulation
the sun will be darkened,
    and the moon will not give its light,

A second characteristic of apocalyptic speech is that some events that have already begun to happen (in the past and present) are cast as a part of the future scheme of things. This mode of writing was meant to assure the readers of the reliability of those parts of the message that really do pertain to the future. For example, Mark's readers can say, "Yes, some families already have broken up and have been divided because some of their members chose to follow Jesus" (vv. 12-13). They can also say, "Yes, 'the desolating abomination' of Roman idols already stands in Jerusalem, where the holy temple once stood" (v. 14). At the same time, what is most important is that they realize that the Lord *will* protect his faithful ones when the end really comes, even shortening the days of distress for the sake of those he has chosen (v. 20). In fact, reports Mark, the most reliable sign of the end of time is yet to come, namely, the glorious return of the Son of Man (to be described in vv. 24-27).

By being in touch with the nature of apocalyptic writing, the readers of chapter 13 can experience the urgency of the early church's waiting and watching for the return of their absent Lord (vv. 15-19). They can also hear Mark's invitation to put aside useless and fearful calculation of deadlines regarding the end of the world, in order to live courageously in the present as discerning and alert missionaries of Jesus' gospel.

13:24-27 The consoling coming of the Son of Man. While apocalyptic writing is recognized by its scary and dark imagery of trials, tribulations, and turmoil in the heavens (vv. 24-25), there is also the consoling light at

²⁵and the stars will be falling from the sky,
and the powers in the heavens will be shaken.
²⁶And then they will see 'the Son of Man coming in the clouds' with great power and glory, ²⁷and then he will send out the angels and gather [his] elect from the four winds, from the end of the earth to the end of the sky.

The Lesson of the Fig Tree. ²⁸"Learn a lesson from the fig tree. When its branch becomes tender and sprouts leaves, you know that summer is near. ²⁹In the same way, when you see these things happening, know that he is near, at the gates. ³⁰Amen, I say to you, this generation will not pass away until all these things have taken place. ³¹Heaven and earth will pass away, but my words will not pass away.

Need for Watchfulness. ³²"But of that day or hour, no one knows, neither the angels in heaven, nor the Son, but only the Father. ³³Be watchful! Be alert! You do not know when the time will come. ³⁴It is like a man traveling abroad. He leaves home and places his servants in charge, each with his work, and orders the gatekeeper to be on the watch. ³⁵Watch, therefore; you do not know when the lord of the house is coming, whether in the evening, or at midnight, or at cockcrow, or in the morning. ³⁶May he not come suddenly and find you sleep-

the heart of it all, which overcomes the darkness. Here that consolation takes the form of the glorious Son of Man, Jesus, coming on the clouds to gather his chosen and faithful ones from all over the earth (vv. 26-27). Mark borrows this encouraging picture of God's deliverance from the promises of the Old Testament prophet Daniel (Dan 7:13-14). Mark's readers today, as well as his first readers, might well be lifted up by this promise of God's final victory over whatever difficulties or darkness envelop them and their world. Encouraged by this hopeful vision, they can accept more readily their responsibilities to be a consoling light for those who may not yet have experienced the hopeful side of the gospel promises.

13:28-37 "We do not know when, but it is near, so persevere!" Just as surely as Jesus' other predictions have come to pass (his death and resurrection, the fall of Jerusalem, the trials his followers would endure), so also will he come again in glory to save his chosen ones. This encouraging message of 13:3-27 concludes with the final call of Jesus to his faithful followers: "The end is near and will happen soon. You will see the signs of the end (vv. 29-31) just as clearly as you see the coming of summer by the new leaves on the fig tree" (vv. 28-29). *"But,"* underlines Mark's Jesus, "since no one knows the day or the hour when the end will come, be watchful and be alert (vv. 32-33). Look around you like the gatekeeper (v. 35). Do not be found sleeping (v. 36), but 'watch!'" (v. 37).

The apocalyptic chapter 13 ends with Mark's sharp challenge for all his readers (not only for Peter, James, John, and Andrew of v. 3). He asks them to persevere in their faith, even in dark days of suffering on behalf of the gospel. It should be clear to Mark's readers that it is their duty to be alert

ing. ³⁷What I say to you, I say to all: 'Watch!' "

14 **The Conspiracy against Jesus.** ¹The Passover and the Feast of Un-leavened Bread were to take place in two days' time. So the chief priests and the scribes were seeking a way to arrest him by treachery and put him to death. ²They

missionaries of that gospel in the present, since the Son of Man entrusted it into their hands until his return in glory.

THE SON OF MAN WILL BE PUT TO DEATH AND WILL RISE THREE DAYS LATER

Mark 14:1–16:8

The very familiar account of the death and resurrection of Jesus is the climax of Mark's involving drama. Everything has been leading to these three chapters, and Mark tells the passion story in such a way that many of the key themes of his Gospel are now drawn together. For example, *the disciples* still fail to have any clear sight or faithful confidence in the Lord they follow. Indeed, they all scatter in the garden when one of them betrays Jesus to his killers with a kiss (14:43-52). Likewise, the alert reader will see how the important images of *bread* and *cup* (developed through chs. 6–8 and 10) come together in the Eucharistic passage that precedes Jesus' agony in the garden (14:22-26). A third developing theme of the earlier chapters, namely, Jesus' identification of himself as the *suffering Son of Man*, finds its climax at the foot of the cross, when the Roman centurion declares at Jesus' death: "Truly this man was the Son of God!" (15:39).

By now, Mark's readers expect some of the developments that occur in these closing chapters. Yet, Mark's passion account also surprises his readers with a very abrupt ending (16:8). When the women leave the tomb and say nothing to anyone because they were afraid (16:8), Mark's readers are left to complete the story with their own careful reflection and response. Why did Mark end the Gospel in this strange way? When did the women overcome their trembling and bewilderment and carry out the mission given to them by the young man at the tomb (16:7)? What about the readers' own hesitation to be courageous proclaimers of Jesus' message? While Mark's readers know that most of Jesus' predictions have come true, two are left unfulfilled. First, did Jesus ever appear to the disciples in Galilee, as he had promised (14:28)? (The reader knows that he did, but *not* from Mark's account.) Second, will Jesus keep his promise to return "in the clouds with great power and glory . . . and gather his elect . . . from the end of the earth

said, "Not during the festival, for fear that there may be a riot among the people."

The Anointing at Bethany. ³When he was in Bethany reclining at table in the house of Simon the leper, a woman came with an alabaster jar of perfumed oil, costly genuine spikenard. She broke the alabaster jar and poured it on his head. ⁴There were some who were indignant. "Why has there been this waste of perfumed oil? ⁵It could have been sold for more than three hundred days' wages and the money given to the poor." They were infuriated with her. ⁶Jesus said, "Let her alone. Why do you make trouble for her? She has done a good thing for me. ⁷The poor you will always have with you, and whenever you wish you can do good to them, but you will not always have me. ⁸She has done what she could. She has anticipated anointing my body for burial. ⁹Amen, I say to you, wherever the gospel is proclaimed to the whole world, what she has done will be told in memory of her."

The Betrayal by Judas. ¹⁰Then Judas Iscariot, one of the Twelve, went off to the chief priests to hand him over to them.

to the end of the sky," as he had promised (13:26-27)? This certainly has not happened yet!

The ending of Mark's Gospel is, therefore, more like the beginning of something else. It is as if Mark is saying that the Gospel is not over yet. In fact, Mark's ending leaves his readers with the startling realization that they have to conclude the Gospel by living out its values. What seemingly began as Mark's account of the *past* life of "Jesus Christ, the Son of God" (1:1) ends with the dramatic invitation that all his readers be faithful imitators of Jesus, the servant Son of Man (10:45), *in the present*, until he comes again to establish the reign of God in power (8:38 and 9:1)!

14:1-11 The preparations for Jesus' death and burial. The first verses of the passion narrative set the scene and the emotional tone for all that is to follow. While the chief priests are afraid to arrest Jesus because "there may be a riot among the people" (v. 2), one of the Twelve makes it easy for them by arranging to hand him over, thereby changing their fear into jubilant anticipation (vv. 10-11). In the midst of the plotting and planning for Jesus' death, Mark places the story of the woman at Bethany (vv. 3-9), whose bold act of reverence for Jesus "will be told in her memory wherever the good news is proclaimed throughout the world."

Typically, those with Jesus do not understand what is going on around them. They fail to see that the woman's act of anointing is the anticipation of Jesus' burial (v. 8). Their intentions are good (the money could be given to the poor, v. 5), but their infuriation with the woman (vv. 4-5) shows that they missed the point of her symbolic action. It should have reminded them of the reality of Jesus' suffering way! Mark does not want *his* readers to miss the point. To care for the poor is a key part of following Jesus (recall the challenge to the rich man in 10:21). But Jesus' followers must also choose

¹¹When they heard him they were pleased and promised to pay him money. Then he looked for an opportunity to hand him over.

Preparations for the Passover. ¹²On the first day of the Feast of Unleavened Bread, when they sacrificed the Passover lamb, his disciples said to him, "Where do you want us to go and prepare for you to eat the Passover?" ¹³He sent two of his disciples and said to them, "Go into the city and a man will meet you, carrying a jar of water. Follow him. ¹⁴Wherever he enters, say to the master of the house, 'The Teacher says, "Where is my guest room where I may eat the Passover with my disciples?" ' ¹⁵Then he will show you a large upper room furnished and ready. Make the preparations for us there." ¹⁶The disciples then went off, entered the city, and found it just as he had told them; and they prepared the Passover.

The Betrayer. ¹⁷When it was evening, he came with the Twelve. ¹⁸And as they reclined at table and were eating, Jesus said, "Amen, I say to you, one of you will betray me, one who is eating with me." ¹⁹They began to be distressed and to say

all that is involved in being his disciples, even to the extent of giving their lives in service of the needs of all, in imitation of the suffering Son of Man (10:44-45).

14:12-26 Jesus makes his own preparations: the Passover Eucharist. Jesus' triumphal entry into Jerusalem (11:8-11) had been preceded by his remarkable prediction that the disciples would find a "colt on which no one has ever sat" (11:2-7). A similarly remarkable prediction precedes the Passover supper that Jesus will celebrate with his disciples (see 14:12-16). Such amazing circumstances prepare Mark's readers for a very special part of the Jesus story.

The Passover meal of the Hebrews celebrated their deliverance from Egypt. ("The Lord will go by, striking down the Egyptians. Seeing the *blood* . . . on the doorposts, the Lord will *pass over* that door and not let the destroyer come into your houses to strike you down," Exod 12:23). As Jesus' Passover meal with his disciples begins, an unnamed (for now) and pitiable disciple is symbolically singled out as the one who will bring about Jesus' betrayal and, ironically, the new deliverance of God's people (vv. 17-21).

Such dramatic preparation leads to Mark's account of the first Eucharistic meal (vv. 22-25), which was as central to his Christian community's life then as it is today. Certainly Mark was faithful in passing on the early church's tradition that the Christian Eucharist is the *new Passover.* Jesus' saving death and resurrection was God's new and perfect way of delivering all people. Mark's Christians shared in the new covenant of Christ's body and blood when they shared the Eucharistic bread and cup! At the same time, Mark uses the occasion of the first Eucharist to round off a special theme he has been developing in regard to the disciples' blindness. (*Bread* has not been mentioned since chapters 6–8, where the disciples did not see the deeper

to him, one by one, "Surely it is not I?" [20]He said to them, "One of the Twelve, the one who dips with me into the dish. [21]For the Son of Man indeed goes, as it is written of him, but woe to that man by whom the Son of Man is betrayed. It would be better for that man if he had never been born."

The Lord's Supper. [22]While they were eating, he took bread, said the blessing, broke it, and gave it to them, and said, "Take it; this is my body." [23]Then he took a cup, gave thanks, and gave it to them, and they all drank from it. [24]He said to them, "This is my blood of the covenant, which will be shed for many. [25]Amen, I say to you, I shall not drink again the fruit of the vine until the day when I drink it new in the kingdom of God." [26]Then,

after singing a hymn, they went out to the Mount of Olives.

Peter's Denial Foretold. [27]Then Jesus said to them, "All of you will have your faith shaken, for it is written:
'I will strike the shepherd,
    and the sheep will be dispersed.'
[28]But after I have been raised up, I shall go before you to Galilee." [29]Peter said to him, "Even though all should have their faith shaken, mine will not be." [30]Then Jesus said to him, "Amen, I say to you, this very night before the cock crows twice you will deny me three times." [31]But he vehemently replied, "Even though I should have to die with you, I will not deny you." And they all spoke similarly.

The Agony in the Garden. [32]Then they came to a place named Gethsemane, and

meaning of Jesus' miracles, especially with "the breads"; *the cup* has not been mentioned since 10:35-45, when Jesus made clear its intimate connection with his death.) Consequently, Mark is telling his readers that those who wish to share in Jesus' Eucharistic cup (now and at the heavenly banquet, v. 25) must first choose to share fully in Jesus' way of suffering service (10:45a: "The Son of Man did not come to be served but to serve"). They must participate actively in Jesus' mission on earth, which involves pouring out their lives "for *many*" (v. 24), always in imitation of him (10:45b: "The Son of Man has come . . . to give his life as ransom *for many*").

14:27-31 "The sheep will be dispersed." After Jesus and his disciples arrive at the Mount of Olives (vv. 26-27), he makes three more predictions: (1) the sheep (his disciples) will be scattered at his death (v. 27); (2) once risen, Jesus will go to Galilee before them (v. 28); and (3) Peter will deny him three times "before the cock crows twice" (v. 30). Despite the protests of Peter and the others, Mark's readers know that two of these predictions will shortly (and sadly) be fulfilled. The disciples will all desert Jesus and flee (v. 50), and Peter will deny him (vv. 66-72). However, the prediction about seeing him in Galilee will be left unfulfilled, even when Mark's Gospel ends (16:8). Mark challenges his readers to ponder the meaning of this unfulfilled prediction as they enter the garden with Jesus, Peter, James, and John (v. 32).

14:32-42 The garden experience: model of radical trust. Mark's account of Jesus' agony in the garden is actually two moving scenes in one. In the

he said to his disciples, "Sit here while I pray." ³³He took with him Peter, James, and John, and began to be troubled and distressed. ³⁴Then he said to them, "My soul is sorrowful even to death. Remain here and keep watch." ³⁵He advanced a little and fell to the ground and prayed that if it were possible the hour might pass by him; ³⁶he said, "Abba, Father, all things are possible to you. Take this cup away from me, but not what I will but what you will." ³⁷When he returned he found them asleep. He said to Peter, "Simon, are you asleep? Could you not keep watch for one hour? ³⁸Watch and pray that you may not undergo the test. The spirit is willing but the flesh is weak." ³⁹Withdrawing again, he prayed, saying the same thing. ⁴⁰Then he returned once more and found them asleep, for they could not keep their eyes open and did not know what to answer him. ⁴¹He returned a third time and said to them, "Are you still sleeping and taking your rest? It is enough. The hour has come. Behold, the Son of Man is to be handed over to sinners. ⁴²Get up, let us go. See, my betrayer is at hand."

The Betrayal and Arrest of Jesus. ⁴³Then, while he was still speaking, Judas, one of the Twelve arrived, accompanied by a crowd with swords and clubs who had come from the chief priests, the scribes, and the elders. ⁴⁴His betrayer had arranged a signal with them, saying, "The man I shall kiss is the one; arrest him and lead him away securely." ⁴⁵He came and immediately went over to him and said,

first (vv. 33-36), Mark's readers are privileged to witness Jesus' profound humanity, as he is overwhelmed by fear and sadness at the prospect of his imminent death (i.e., the cup of v. 36). They also recognize in his final acceptance of his Father's will the ultimate act of his loving humanity, i.e., his choice to give up his life for the Father and for all people.

The second scene (vv. 37-42) focuses the readers' attention on the disciples who fall asleep as Jesus struggles in prayer. Mark hopes that his readers will face life and choose to be human like Jesus, not like the disciples. The profundity of Jesus' choice to take the cup can be grasped, ironically, only by certain readers of Mark's Gospel—that is, only those who have come as close to despair as Jesus did in the garden can really identify with him. Mark hopes that Jesus will be for them a realistic (truly human) model of trust and love in their painful "hour" (v. 41) of Christian and human life!

14:43-52 It all starts to fall into place: the betrayal and arrest. Once Jesus has made the decision to give himself up to his Father's will (v. 36), the other pieces of the passion account quickly fall into place. Immediately after Jesus is betrayed by the kiss of Judas (vv. 44-45), he is arrested and led off as if he were a common robber (v. 48). Mark makes it clear, in verse 49, that the arrest of the innocent Jesus, like the rest of his passion experience, is in accord with Old Testament prophecies about the way the Messiah of Israel would be treated by his own people.

Three other details in the passage bring out how oblivious Jesus' companions are to what is really happening. One of them thinks he can stop

The Mount of Olives from the east wall of Jerusalem

Jerusalem as seen from the Mount of Olives

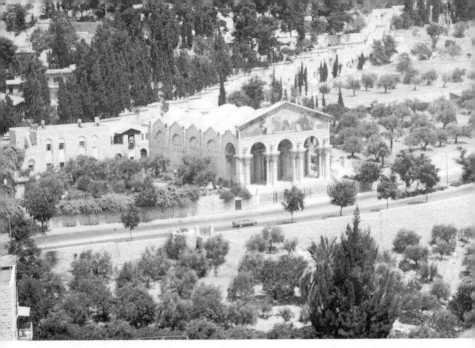

The Basilica of the Agony, also called the Church of All Nations, marking the site of Christ's agony in the adjoining Garden of Gethsemani (Mark 14:32ff.).

The Grotto of Gethsemani, traditionally believed to be the cave in which Judas betrayed Jesus and where Jesus was arrested

"Rabbi." And he kissed him. ⁴⁶At this they laid hands on him and arrested him. ⁴⁷One of the bystanders drew his sword, struck the high priest's servant, and cut off his ear. ⁴⁸Jesus said to them in reply, "Have you come out as against a robber, with swords and clubs, to seize me? ⁴⁹Day after day I was with you teaching in the temple area, yet you did not arrest me; but that the scriptures may be fulfilled." ⁵⁰And they all left him and fled. ⁵¹Now a young man followed him wearing nothing but a linen cloth about his body. They seized him, ⁵²but he left the cloth behind and ran off naked.

Jesus before the Sanhedrin. ⁵³They led Jesus away to the high priest, and all the chief priests and the elders and the scribes came together. ⁵⁴Peter followed him at a distance into the high priest's courtyard and was seated with the guards, warming himself at the fire. ⁵⁵The chief priests and the entire Sanhedrin kept trying to obtain testimony against Jesus in order to put him to death, but they found none.

⁵⁶Many gave false witness against him, but their testimony did not agree. ⁵⁷Some took the stand and testified falsely against him, alleging, ⁵⁸"We heard him say, 'I will destroy this temple made with hands and within three days I will build another not made with hands.'" ⁵⁹Even so their testimony did not agree. ⁶⁰The high priest rose before the assembly and questioned Jesus, saying, "Have you no answer? What are these men testifying against you?" ⁶¹But he was silent and answered nothing. Again the high priest asked him and said to him, "Are you the Messiah, the son of the Blessed One?" ⁶²Then Jesus answered, "I am;

and 'you will see the Son of Man
  seated at the right hand of the Power
  and coming with the clouds of
  heaven.'"

⁶³At that the high priest tore his garments and said, "What further need have we of witnesses? ⁶⁴You have heard the blasphemy. What do you think?" They all condemned him as deserving to die.

violence with violence (v. 47). All the rest leave him alone (v. 50). And even the young man who does follow, "wearing nothing but a linen cloth," runs away as soon as Jesus' enemies try to seize him (vv. 51-52). These details of Mark's passion account serve not only to recall for his readers "the way it all happened" but also to stimulate them to ask themselves how far they would go in staying with Jesus and his gospel values in their own difficult life situations.

14:53-65 The trial and the verdict and the sentence: Death! The so-called trial of Jesus is full of false and trumped-up charges against him. In response to such testimony, Jesus "was silent and answered nothing" (v. 61). The high priest's verdict of guilty (v. 64) comes only when the "silent one" does acknowledge that he is "the Messiah, the Son of the Blessed One," who will sit with God ("the Power") in the heavens, and who will "come with the clouds of heaven" as judge in the last days (v. 62). It is ironic that none of the *false* testimony can disprove Jesus' innocence (v. 55). It is only when he speaks *the truth* about himself that he is condemned to death (v. 62)! Certainly Mark's readers would be proud of their Lord's perseverance in the face of this humiliating trial and the mocking taunts and spittle that accompany

⁶⁵Some began to spit on him. They blindfolded him and struck him and said to him, "Prophesy!" And the guards greeted him with blows.

Peter's Denial of Jesus. ⁶⁶While Peter was below in the courtyard, one of the high priest's maids came along. ⁶⁷Seeing Peter warming himself, she looked intently at him and said, "You too were with the Nazarene, Jesus." ⁶⁸But he denied it saying, "I neither know nor understand what you are talking about." So he went out into the outer court. [Then the cock crowed.] ⁶⁹The maid saw him and began again to say to the bystanders, "This man is one of them." ⁷⁰Once again he denied it. A little later the bystanders said to Peter once more, "Surely you are one of them; for you too are a Galilean." ⁷¹He began to curse and to swear, "I do not know this man about whom you are talking." ⁷²And immediately a cock crowed a second time. Then Peter remembered the word that Jesus had said to him, "Before the cock crows twice you will deny me three times." He broke down and wept.

15 **Jesus before Pilate.** ¹As soon as morning came, the chief priests with the elders and the scribes, that is, the whole Sanhedrin, held a council. They bound Jesus, led him away, and handed him over to Pilate. ²Pilate questioned him, "Are you the king of the Jews?" He said to him in reply, "You say so." ³The chief priests accused him of many things. ⁴Again Pilate questioned him, "Have you no answer? See how many things they accuse you of." ⁵Jesus gave him no further answer, so that Pilate was amazed.

it (v. 65). But will they be any more faithful to him than Peter was (see the next passage) when their faith is severely tested?

14:66-72 Peter denies Jesus three times. As Jesus had predicted (14:27), all his disciples deserted him in the garden and fled (14:50). As he had predicted (14:30), even Peter denies him, not once but three times (vv. 66-72). Peter's tears (v. 72) indicate his remorse, however, and his sorrow could be encouraging to any of Mark's readers who may at times have been unfaithful followers of Jesus. For they know that the one who denied his Lord three times would go on to experience the mercy of a forgiving God and become the early church's greatest apostle among the Jews (Gal 2:8) after the resurrection. Through the tears of Peter, Mark offers a great deal of hope to any of his Christian readers who lack courage and trust. It is never too late for them to say with contrite hearts: "Yes, *I am with* the Nazarene, Jesus!"

15:1-15 The chief priests and Pilate hand over "the king of the Jews." It is clear from the start of this passage (15:1: "As soon as morning came") how anxious the Jewish priests are to get the cooperation of the Roman official, Pilate, in putting Jesus away. Earlier the high priest had asked Jesus, in Jewish terms, if he was "the Messiah, the Son of the Blessed One." The Roman now asks, in terms that have political meaning for him, if Jesus is "the king of the Jews" (15:2). Jesus accepts the title given him by Pilate (15:3), which is the equivalent of saying "guilty" to the charge of high treason. (There is no king in Roman territory but Caesar!) Even so, Pilate sees through the

The Sentence of Death. [6]Now on the occasion of the feast he used to release to them one prisoner whom they requested. [7]A man called Barabbas was then in prison along with the rebels who had committed murder in a rebellion. [8]The crowd came forward and began to ask him to do for them as he was accustomed. [9]Pilate answered, "Do you want me to release to you the king of the Jews?" [10]For he knew that it was out of envy that the chief priests had handed him over. [11]But the chief priests stirred up the crowd to have him release Barabbas for them instead. [12]Pilate again said to them in reply, "Then what [do you want] me to do with [the man you call] the king of the Jews?" [13]They shouted again, "Crucify him." [14]Pilate said to them, "Why? What evil has he done?" They only shouted the louder, "Crucify him." [15]So Pilate, wishing to satisfy the crowd, released Barabbas to them and, after he had Jesus scourged, handed him over to be crucified.

Mockery by the Soldiers. [16]The soldiers led him away inside the palace, that is, the praetorium, and assembled the whole cohort. [17]They clothed him in purple and, weaving a crown of thorns, placed it on him. [18]They began to salute him with, "Hail, King of the Jews!" [19]and kept striking his head with a reed and spitting upon him. They knelt before him in homage. [20]And when they had mocked him, they stripped him of the purple cloak, dressed him in his own clothes, and led him out to crucify him.

The Way of the Cross. [21]They pressed into service a passer-by, Simon, a Cyrenian, who was coming in from the country, the father of Alexander and Rufus, to carry his cross.

The Crucifixion. [22]They brought him to the place of Golgotha (which is translated Place of the Skull). [23]They gave him

charges made against Jesus (15:10: "He knew, of course, that it was out of envy that the chief priests had handed him over"). He tries to release Jesus instead of Barabbas, but the priests influence the crowd to ask for Barabbas (v. 11). Pilate ends up "wishing to satisfy the crowd," which calls for Jesus' death: "Crucify him!" (vv. 11-15). In so doing, Pilate plays out his cowardly role in the Gospel drama. Though convinced of Jesus' innocence, he still yields to pressure and hands him over to be scourged and crucified. And Jesus begins to drink deeply from "the cup."

15:20-32 The climax: they mocked and crucified him. Once again, after the intrigue of "the trials" that shows how innocent Jesus really is, the horrible events of the passion quickly unfold. After Jesus is scourged (v. 15), he is dressed "in purple" and "crowned" with thorns by the Roman soldiers, who mockingly call him "King of the Jews" (vv. 16-20). Through all the spitting and the beating he receives, Jesus remains silent. Mark's readers would certainly recognize in this the fulfillment of the Isaian prophecy concerning the Messiah: "I gave my back to those who beat me. . . . My face I did not shield from buffets and spitting" (Isa 50:6).

The climax of the Markan drama comes in Jesus' crucifixion. The readers of Mark's Gospel will notice that some familiar details are missing as they read Mark's account of the way of the cross. For example, the lamenting

wine drugged with myrrh, but he did not take it. ²⁴Then they crucified him and divided his garments by casting lots for them to see what each should take. ²⁵It was nine o'clock in the morning when they crucified him. ²⁶The inscription of the charge against him read, "The King of the Jews." ²⁷With him they crucified two revolutionaries, one on his right and one on his left.[²⁸] ²⁹Those passing by reviled him, shaking their heads and saying, "Aha! You who would destroy the temple and rebuild it in three days, ³⁰save yourself by coming down from the cross." ³¹Likewise the chief priests, with the scribes, mocked him among themselves and said, "He saved others; he cannot save himself. ³²Let the Messiah, the King of Israel, come down now from the cross that we may see and believe." Those who were crucified with him also kept abusing him.

The Death of Jesus. ³³At noon darkness came over the whole land until three in the afternoon. ³⁴And at three o'clock Jesus cried out in a loud voice, *"Eloi, Eloi, lema sabachthani?"* which is translated, "My God, my God, why have you forsaken me?" ³⁵Some of the bystanders who heard it said, "Look, he is calling Elijah."

women of Jerusalem (Luke 23:27-31) do not meet him on the way. Likewise, *both* of the men who are crucified with Jesus join the passers-by in taunting Jesus (vv. 27-32), unlike what is recorded by Luke in the memorable exchange between Jesus and the "good thief" (Luke 23:40-43). Consequently, Mark's readers are left with the starkest of pictures. Their Lord hangs alone on the cross, exposed to the mockery of the people he came to save.

One of the last cries of mockery (v. 32: "Let the Messiah, 'the King of Israel,' come down now from the cross that we may see and believe") becomes for Mark a profound challenge to his readers' faith. Will they believe in Jesus precisely because he did *not* come down from the cross? Will they be able to see meaning in their own inexplicable suffering in the light of the absurd suffering of their Messiah and King? Will they be able to see the positive, saving value of their suffering as St. Paul did: "In my flesh I am filling up what is lacking in the afflictions of Christ on behalf of his body, the church" (Col 1:24)?

15:33-41 In his death Jesus is seen as the Son of God. Mark's readers have now come with Jesus to *the* moment that all his life has prepared for. Along with Jesus' "blind" disciples, they have walked with Jesus as he has shared life and healing power with others (chs. 1–8). They have learned what is necessary to be enlightened and true Christian disciples (chs. 9–13). All that is needed now is for them to stay with him to the end!

It is in the dark hour of Jesus' death (v. 33) that Mark's readers see the light. It is there, at the foot of the cross, that they hear their Lord's cry, "My God, my God, why have you forsaken me?" (v. 34). Mark does not want his Christians to mistake Jesus' cry for what it is not (as did the bystanders, who thought it was simply a desperate appeal for Elijah's help, vv. 35-36).

³⁶One of them ran, soaked a sponge with wine, put it on a reed, and gave it to him to drink, saying, "Wait, let us see if Elijah comes to take him down." ³⁷Jesus gave a loud cry and breathed his last. ³⁸The veil of the sanctuary was torn in two from top to bottom. ³⁹When the centurion who stood facing him saw how he breathed his last he said, "Truly this man was the Son of God!" ⁴⁰There were also women looking on from a distance. Among them were Mary Magdalene, Mary the mother of the younger James and of Joses, and Salome. ⁴¹These women had followed him when he was in Galilee and ministered to him. There were also many other women who had come up with him to Jerusalem.

The Burial of Jesus. ⁴²When it was already evening, since it was the day of preparation, the day before the sabbath, ⁴³Joseph of Arimathea, a distinguished member of the council, who was himself awaiting the kingdom of God, came and courageously went to Pilate and asked for the body of Jesus. ⁴⁴Pilate was amazed that he was already dead. He summoned the centurion and asked him if Jesus had already died. ⁴⁵And when he learned of it from the centurion, he gave the body to Joseph. ⁴⁶Having bought a linen cloth, he took him down, wrapped him in the linen cloth and laid him in a tomb that had been hewn out of the rock. Then he rolled a stone against the entrance to the

Rather, he wants them to recognize in Jesus' last words and death the ultimate act of self-giving and trust. Like the Psalmist who first uttered this cry (Ps 22:2), Mark's Jesus believes that God will hear him (Ps 22:25) and will give him life, precisely because he suffered and died out of love and obedience! Who would ever believe that life could come from death? Yet Mark wants his readers to believe that this *is* true, not only for Jesus but also for anyone who will follow in his steps. Who would expect a Gentile centurion to be the first to declare that Jesus is "the Son of God"? Yet Mark asks his readers to see the *living* Son of God most clearly in his humble and loving *death*, just as the pagan centurion did.

15:42-47 Jesus is buried by Joseph of Arimathea. Near the end of Jesus' ministry in Jerusalem, he had met with a scribe who was "not far from the kingdom of God" (12:28-34). For Mark's readers, that scribe's sincere response to Jesus was more authentic than the response of Jesus' own disciples. Once again, in the burial scene, it is not Jesus' disciples who respond properly, but Joseph of Arimathea, "a distinguished member of the council" (15:43). He was bold enough to take reverent care of Jesus' burial (vv. 43-46). Thus, even as he relates the account of Jesus' burial, Mark prods his readers to have more faith than Jesus' first disciples. Pilate's inquiry as to whether Jesus was already dead (v. 44) also becomes an important detail for Mark. Such insistence on finality prepares Mark's readers for the most striking reversal of the entire Gospel, namely, the proclamation of the young man at the tomb: "Do not be amazed! You seek Jesus of Nazareth, the crucified. He *has been raised*; he is not here. Behold the place where they laid him" (16:6).

tomb. ⁴⁷Mary Magdalene and Mary the mother of Joses watched where he was laid.

16 **The Resurrection of Jesus.** ¹When the sabbath was over, Mary Magdalene, Mary, the mother of James, and Salome bought spices so that they might go and anoint him. ²Very early when the sun had risen, on the first day of the week, they came to the tomb. ³They were saying to one another, "Who will roll back the stone for us from the entrance to the tomb?" ⁴When they looked up, they saw that the stone had been rolled back; it was very large. ⁵On entering the tomb they saw a young man sitting on the right side, clothed in a white robe, and they were utterly amazed. ⁶He said to them, "Do not be amazed! You seek Jesus of Nazareth, the crucified. He has been raised; he is not here. Behold the place where they laid him. ⁷But go and tell his disciples and Peter, 'He is going before you to Galilee; there you will see him, as he told you.'" ⁸Then they went out and fled from the tomb, seized with trembling and bewilderment. They said nothing to anyone, for they were afraid.

16:1-8 The end is the beginning! Go now and tell that he is risen! "They said nothing to anyone, for they were afraid" (16:8). This is how the women respond to the wonderful news of Jesus' resurrection. This is also how Mark ends his Gospel. (It is generally agreed that verses 9-20 were added to Mark's Gospel later by those who could not believe that Mark would end it as he did!) By ending it this way, Mark actually invites his readers to step in and take the place of the women at the empty tomb. The women failed to carry out the mission orders they received from God's messenger (the young man "clothed in a white robe," v. 5). Mark wants his disciples, men and women, to spread the good news that God has brought life from death by raising Jesus from the dead (vv. 6-7). He wants them to do so without the fear, bewilderment, or trembling of the three women at the tomb (v. 8).

Mark's readers might well ask how they could be any better as disciples than the women and men who were with Jesus during his life, at his death, and at the empty tomb. Mark would probably answer this way: "It is for you that this Gospel has been written! Persevere as faithful followers of the Jesus I have presented to you. His resurrection is not the end! He has gone ahead of you as the servant Messiah. Now you must care for the needs of those most in need, until he comes again. He has given meaning to suffering and has brought life from death. Trust in him and give his life to those who have no hope. Whatever you do, let others know by your courageous words and your lives of service that you have heard the Lord's call and that you have chosen to follow his lead until you see him, as he has promised."

THE LONGER ENDING

The Appearance to Mary Magdalene.
[⁹When he had risen, early on the first day of the week, he appeared first to Mary Magdalene, out of whom he had driven seven demons. ¹⁰She went and told his companions who were mourning and weeping. ¹¹When they heard that he was alive and had been seen by her, they did not believe.

The Appearance to Two Disciples.
¹²After this he appeared in another form to two of them walking along on their way to the country. ¹³They returned and told the others; but they did not believe them either.

The Commissioning of the Eleven.
¹⁴[But] later, as the eleven were at table, he appeared to them and rebuked them for their unbelief and hardness of heart

THE THREE "OTHER ENDINGS" OF THE GOSPEL

16:9-20 +

Although virtually all of today's scholars of the Bible believe that Mark had a purpose in ending his Gospel abruptly at 16:8, this was not always the case. Some first- or second-century Christians tried to "complete" his Gospel drama by adding scenes that they thought Mark should have added himself.

The first extra ending, the so-called *Longer Ending* (vv. 9-20), includes appearances of the risen Jesus to Mary Magdalene and to the disciples. These visions were meant to inspire the early missionary church to "go into the whole world and proclaim the gospel to every creature" (v. 15). The church's missionaries had nothing to fear, because the ascended Lord (v. 19) was with them in their preaching (v. 20) and would confirm their message with special signs of his protection and power (vv. 17-18). Alert readers will notice some themes in these verses that are unlike anything they have seen before in Mark's Gospel. They may also recognize in them echoes of familiar scenes from the other Gospels, gathered together to round off Mark's abrupt ending (for example, Mary Magdalene meets with Jesus alone in John's Gospel, 20:11-18; the appearance to the two disciples is reminiscent of Luke's Emmaus appearance, 24:13-35; and the commission to "go into the whole world to preach" sounds like the ending of Matthew's Gospel, 28:16-20).

The so-called *Shorter Ending*, when read immediately after 16:8, was another attempt of the early church to end Mark's Gospel more smoothly. It reverses the fear and silence of the women at the tomb and shows how the message of the resurrection came to be proclaimed through "Peter's companions."

The *Freer Ending*, preserved in the Freer Gallery in Washington, D.C., is a fifth-century addition to the Longer Ending. Appearing between verses

because they had not believed those who saw him after he had been raised. [15]He said to them, "Go into the whole world and proclaim the gospel to every creature. [16]Whoever believes and is baptized will be saved; whoever does not believe will be condemned. [17]These signs will accompany those who believe: in my name they will drive out demons, they will speak new languages. [18]They will pick up serpents [with their hands], and if they drink any deadly thing, it will not harm them. They will lay hands on the sick, and they will recover."

The Ascension of Jesus. [19]So then the Lord Jesus, after he spoke to them, was taken up into heaven and took his seat at the right hand of God. [20]But they went forth and preached everywhere, while the Lord worked with them and confirmed the word through accompanying signs.]

THE SHORTER ENDING

[And they reported all the instructions briefly to Peter's companions. Afterwards Jesus himself, through them, sent forth from east to west the sacred and imperishable proclamation of eternal salvation. Amen.]

14 and 15, it excuses the disbelief and stubbornness of the disciples found at 16:14.

Although the church has recognized these "added endings" as worthy of inclusion in the inspired text, none of them is as inspiring and involving as Mark's own. Mark's abrupt ending leaves it up to his readers to "complete" his Gospel in their lives.

REVIEW AIDS AND DISCUSSION TOPICS

I

Introduction (pages 7–12)

1. After reading the whole Gospel of Mark, with whom did you identify most? (With Jesus? With the disciples? With some other character?) Why?
2. In a phrase or two, how would you describe Mark's "portrait" of Jesus? Of his disciples? Which scene(s) best exemplify this for you?
3. Why is the scene in the garden (14:32-42) such an important passage?
4. Which "cycle" of Sunday readings features Mark's Gospel? Which "cycle" and whose Gospel are featured on Sundays at the present time?
5. Who was Mark, the inspired author of this Gospel? Why did he write such a fast-paced and demanding Gospel? What did he mean to symbolize by his use of "Galilee" in his Gospel?
6. After the experience of reading Mark's Gospel, along with the Preface and Introduction, what impresses or interests you the most?

II

1:1–5:43 The Drama Begins: Who Is Jesus? (pages 13–36)

1. Even in the first chapter of his Gospel, Mark already hints as to how his "Jesus drama" will end. List a few of those hints. How does the so-called "messianic secret" theme contribute to the Gospel's development?
2. According to Mark (chs. 1–5), what were some characteristic responses of various people to Jesus' teaching and miracles? What did the people expect Jesus to be for them? On the other hand, who was Mark's Jesus for them? And what response did Mark's Jesus seek from them? Today, what do people want Jesus to be like for them? What does Mark's Jesus want from you and from today's church?
3. Which scene (miracle story, conflict passage, parable, etc.) stands out for you as a highlight of the first five chapters of the Gospel? Why? How does your "highlight passage" fit into the developing drama of Mark's Gospel? What did it mean to Mark's first readers?

III

6:1–8:26 Of Bread and Blindness: Who Is Jesus? (pages 36–48)

1. How many scenes in chapters 6 to 8 of Mark's Gospel allude to bread (food, loaves)? What do these bread scenes reveal about Jesus' identity? About God's care for his people, past and present?
2. How were the various miracle stories of chapters 6 to 8 (for example, the Syro-Phoenician's daughter and the deaf-mute of chapter 7 and the blind man of chapter 8) meant to involve the first readers of Mark's Gospel in A.D. 70? How does Mark's Jesus want his people to "hear" and "see" him today, in the twentieth century?

3. What does participation in the Eucharist mean to you? How is it meant to alleviate the "blindness" of God's people, according to Mark?

IV

8:27–10:52 Jesus Is "the Messiah"! What Is His Way? (pages 49–62)

1. Which teaching of Mark's Jesus about his way affects you the most personally? Why? How do you respond? Can you express your feelings in prayer?

2. Which of Jesus' teachings affects people close to you? How can you be a source of challenge or comfort to them? How can you do so in some concrete way soon?

3. Which of Jesus' teachings about his way does the church need to hear today? How can you help make this message heard (in your local community, parish, diocese, etc.)?

V

11:1–13:37 On to Jerusalem — This Is His Way! (pages 62–76)

1. List a few of the many contrasts that appear in chapters 11 and 12 (for example, the people's response to Jesus, 11:9, versus the response of the chief priests, 11:18). Which of these passages raises an issue that you consider to be of great importance in the life of the church today? Why?

2. What is *apocalyptic language?* When and why is it employed? What purpose did Mark have in presenting Jesus' apocalyptic speech (ch. 13) as he does? What message does chapter 13 hold out to today's Christian?

VI

14:1–16:8 Of Death and Resurrection Life (pages 76–88)

1. Mark records many dramatic scenes as Jesus prepares for his death. Which scene(s) involved you the most? Why?

2. How is the Christian Eucharist related to the Hebrew Passover? What is similar in the meaning of these celebrations? How do they differ? How do the Markan themes of *bread* and *cup* help define the meaning of Eucharist for the readers of his Gospel?

3. What is *the* climax of Mark's Gospel? Explain why this is so.

4. Compare the resurrection account and the ending of Mark's Gospel (16:1-8) with Matthew's (28:1-20) and Luke's (24:1-50). Why did Mark end his Gospel as he did? Would you have ended it differently? How? How can you step in to do what the women were "too afraid" to do?

5. How are Mark's Jesus and Mark's whole Gospel like a parable? (See the comment on 4:1-34 for a definition and the meaning of parables.)